THE PRESENCE OF GOD IN PASTORAL COUNSELING

THE PRESENCE OF GOD IN PASTORAL COUNSELING

Wayne E. Oates

WORD BOOKS
PUBLISHER
WACO, TEXAS
A DIVISION OF
WORD, INCORPORATED

Library of Congress Cataloging in Publication Data

Oates, Wayne Edward, 1917–
  The presence of God in pastoral counseling.

  Bibliography: p.
  1. Pastoral counseling.   2. God—Omnipresence.
I. Title.
BV4012.Q235 1986   253.5   86–18998
ISBN 0–8499–0475–7

Printed in the United States of America

67898 BKC 987654321

To
Ralph Bonacker
My mentor and pastoral supervisor

Contents

Preface

Pastoral counseling has its roots in both worship and science. Too often, the scientific exploration of interpersonal relations has been the most apparent. Recently, however, the worship dimension of pastoral counseling has become more evident. In this book, I am concentrating on the centrality of the Presence of God in the day-to-day work of pastoral counselors.

I do this with some reticence because the experience of the Presence of God is ineffable. Words will not encompass it; they only point to the reality that is God. Yet words must be used and with the hope and prayer that they will not obscure but clarify our struggle to "know even as we are known by God."

In this writing, I am indebted to my colleagues, Henlee Barnette and James Hyde, for reading the manuscript and making meaningful suggestions for its clarity and content. I am especially grateful for the expert colleagueship with my research assistant, Mrs. Jenni Khaliel, for her research and manuscript preparation skills.

Wayne E. Oates
University of Louisville
School of Medicine

Some Meanings of the Presence of God

1
Some Meanings of the Presence of God

The meanings of the Presence of God upon which I build the assumptions and conclusions of this book are drawn from Judaeo-Christian teachings. At no point, however, do I disparage the meanings of the Presence found in Eastern or any other form of religion. Rather, pastoral counseling in its modern forms has been birthed, nurtured, and brought to its present very young adulthood in the context of the Judaeo-Christian tradition.

When we as pastoral counselors have called upon explicitly religious teachings, more often than not they have come from this source. Ordinarily, when we have rebelled against our religious heritage, we have rebelled against some variant of the Christian tradition.

If we have rebelled against the spiritual vacuum of a secular upbringing to become religious, often we have become Christians. If, now, we are hesitant to speak "god-talk" with ourselves, our counselees, and our colleagues, it is usually the Judaeo-Christian "god-talk" we blush to speak. When we utilize religious categories, they tend to be from Judaeo-Christian belief systems, as well.

Therefore, I have chosen to write specifically about the meanings of the Presence of God that we draw from the Old and New Testaments and from Christian history. It is important to be clear about what the Presence of God does not mean as well as what it does mean.

WHAT IS NOT MEANT BY THE PRESENCE OF GOD

American commercialism, propaganda, advertising—with the express aim of making money—has one particular trait that reminds one of the Eternal God: it is no respecter of persons or topics. In this discussion, I do not mean by the Presence of God the crass images of God prevalent today, as in every generation, in such phrases as "I've found it," with "it" referring to God and/or Jesus Christ. I would prefer to write about these misappropriations of the Presence of God as magic and/or superstition. Such off-centerings of the most profound intentions of the human heart were more aptly named idolatry in prophetic writings.

Yet, I do have empathy for the person or persons whom I hear speaking this way of God or Jesus Christ. I have a painful awareness of the eras in my own life when I placed other idols at the center of my affections. I have had to repent and cast away every high thing that exalted itself against the knowledge of the Living God. Any time I point the finger of criticism at these peddlers of this or that gospel, three other fingers are pointing back at me. After all, I *do* hope that you, or the library, or the friend from whom you have borrowed this book did actually *buy* this book! Who am I to cast stones at commercialism?

Similarly, many of us pastoral counselors have been pushed against the economic wall of necessity by the lack of support from churches. We have organized extensive and complex counseling centers, an American Association of Pastoral Counselors, with well-organized regional groups. We have to charge fees, either for our organizations or, in the cases of those in "private practice," for ourselves. We have had to seek charitable subsidies. Now, pastoral counseling organizations are in many instances pushing hard for state certifications in order to qualify for third-party payments by medical insurance companies for services as "health providers." These concerns have pushed some of us into risky and highly dubious ethical and legal quandaries. When, therefore, we speak of "commercialism," we need be aware that those who live in glass houses should not throw stones.

Suffice it to say here, then, that we are *not* speaking of the Presence of God as a private possession of an individual or group. We are *not,* as Browning said, speaking of the Presence of God as a "purveyor to men's appetites." I am not speaking of God as if I were a Greek worshiping Hygeia, the daughter of Asclepius, the god of health. Nor am I, therefore, speaking of pastoral counseling as *ultimately* concerned with "health delivery" and third-party payments of insurance companies.

WHAT THE PRESENCE OF GOD DOES MEAN

THE GENERAL, INESCAPABLE PRESENCE OF GOD

The Presence of God is portrayed in Psalm 139 as all-pervasive and all-knowing of humankind's thoughts and doings. The Psalmist says: "Thou searchest out my path and my lying down, and art acquainted with all my ways. . . . Whither shall I go from thy Spirit?" (Psalm 139:3, 7).

Jesus' disciples asked Him, "Lord, to whom [else] shall we go?" (John 6:68). He had encompassed them with His Presence. Wherever they went, they would see Him in the faces and forms of the people they met.

This general and inescapable Presence of God is portrayed in Francis Thompson's "The Hound of Heaven":

> Up vistaed hopes I sped;
> And shot, precipitated,
> Adown Titanic glooms of chasmed fears,
> From those strong Feet that followed, followed after.
> But with unhurrying chase,
> And unperturbed pace,
> Deliberate speed, majestic instancy,
> They beat—and a Voice beat
> More instant than the Feet—
> "All things betray thee, who betrayest Me." [1]

This general, inescapable Presence of God is also biblically portrayed in the very creation itself, in our *umwelt* of the natural

universe. "The heavens are telling the glory of God . . ." (Psalm
19:1). "Know that the Lord is God! It is he that made us, and
we are his . . ." (Psalm 100:3). "And he made from one every
nation of men to live on all the face of the earth, having determined allotted periods and the boundaries of their habitation,
that they should seek God, in the hope that they might feel
after him and find him. Yet he is not far from each one of us,
for 'In him we live and move and have our being'. . ." (Acts
17:26–28a). This same kind of perception of God is partially
evident in pantheism, but the biblical meaning of the Presence
of God in creation is not pantheistic. God is always portrayed
as other than, different from, and sovereign over His creation.
To worship His creation is to "exchange the truth about God
for a lie and to worship and serve the creature rather than the
Creator . . ." (Romans 1:25). This understanding of the sover-
eignty of God in creation is explored more fully in the next
chapter.

The Presence of God As "Dwelling with Humankind"

The word *Shekinah* is not in the Bible. It was first used in
the Targums, or the Aramaic translations of the Scriptures, partic-
ularly the Pentateuch. It was a part of the oral rather than the
written tradition. Nevertheless, it is a very rich word used to
refer very cautiously and reverently to the Presence of God in
His choosing to dwell with us as His creatures. It is found in
close companionship with another meaning of the Presence of
God, "the glory of God." The Targums on Isaiah 6:1–5 say:
"I saw the glory (*yekara*) of the Lord resting on his throne—
my eyes have seen the glory (*yekara*) of the Shekinah of the
Lord."

Among the Israelites, the Shekinah of God was apparent to
Moses in the burning bush, in the Ark of the Covenant, in the
Temple. In the New Testament, the dwelling of God in the Lord
Jesus Christ is the focus of the Presence of God. "The Word
became flesh and dwelt among us, full of grace and truth; we
have beheld his glory, glory as of the only Son of the Father"
(John 1:14). Three of the terms in this text are found in the
Aramaic Targums: "The Word" (*memra*), "dwelt" (*Shekinah*),

and "glory" (*yekara*). The whole Fourth Gospel concentrates on the gospel of the glory of God in Jesus Christ dwelling among us. The indwelling of the Holy Spirit, the Father, and the Son is vividly stated in John 14:16–17, 23: And I will pray the Father, and he will give you another Counselor, to be with you for ever, even the Spirit of Truth . . . you know him, for he dwells with you, and will be in you. . . . If a man loves me, he will keep my word, and my Father will love him, and we will come to him and make our home with him.' "

The meaning of the Presence of God as dwelling with us is both eschatological and apocalyptic in the New Testament as we see in Revelation 21:3–4: ". . . and I heard a great voice from the throne saying, 'Behold, the dwelling of God is with men. He will dwell with them, and they shall be his people, and God himself shall be with them; and he will wipe away every tear from their eyes, and death shall be no more, neither shall there be mourning nor crying nor pain any more, for the former things have passed away.' "

The meaning of God as dwelling with us, making His home with us, is prefaced in Jesus' promise when He says: "I will not leave you desolate [or, as orphans]; I will come to you" (John 14:18). This meaning is extremely relevant to the day-to-day work of the pastoral counselor. Repeatedly we meet people who are indeed desolate, orphaned more often by psychological and spiritual deprivation, abandonment, rejection, or domination than by the death of family members. To many who come to see us, our counseling room is the nearest thing to home or church they have. It is a "dwelling place." Our presence is far more than the donning of a ministerial "role." It is, whether we are comfortable with the reality or not, the *promise* of the Presence of God, not only to them but also to us.

THE PRESENCE OF GOD IN A PEOPLE WITH A CLEAR IDENTITY

The Shekinah of the Lord—i.e., the Presence of God with people—gives us a special covenanted relationship with each other. We become the "people of God." God gives a people His name, as He did to Moses. Ruth had become dispossessed of a "people" in the death of her husband, Naomi's son. When she

left her people to go with Naomi, she was all the more bereft
of a "people." Orpah, Ruth's sister-in-law, returned to her people.
But Ruth said: "Entreat me not to leave you or to return from
following you; for where you go I will go, and where you lodge
I will lodge; your people shall be my people, and your God
my God . . ." (1:16). She chose not only Naomi as a mentor,
but also chose her God and people. This became her identity.
Out of it grew her individuality.

When we as Christians enter into the new covenant of the
redemption of Jesus Christ as Lord, 1 Peter 2:9–10 says to us:
"But you are a chosen race, a royal priesthood, a holy nation,
God's own people, that you may declare the wonderful deeds
of him who called you out of darkness into his marvelous light.
Once you were no people but now you are God's people."

Increasingly in pastoral counseling, the isolated care of an individual is being found helpful but incomplete. A community of
concern, of faith, and free of pretense is needed. As Howard
Clinebell says: "It is in communities of mutual caring that the
fullest possible liberation of spiritual potentials takes place." [2]
L. C. Marsh, a psychiatrist who experimented with inspirational
community formation in a large mental hospital, coined the
maxim: "By the crowd they have been broken; by the crowd
shall they be healed." Alan Paton, speaking of the plight of South
Africa, said that the counselors of South Africa have counsel
for many things, except for one: the brokenness of its people.
Pastoral counseling in American life is in much the same situation.
The helpless, treadmill life of poverty and welfare families; the
ingrownness of privileged elite families; the substitution of drugs,
alcohol, and depression for a community of faith; a genuine sense
of being apart from and without people—all these call for an
agonizing reappraisal of how an individual, a family, or a class
of estranged people find an identity that enables them who are
not a people to become the people of God. The Presence of
God in the Body of Christ, the "peoplehood" of faith, is the
garment whose hem we in pastoral counseling greatly need to
touch—and to be touched by its Master! Maybe our concern
with systems approaches will bring more of us out of our isolation.
A painful reappraisal of our awareness or lack of awareness of
the Presence of God in a community will do so even more surely.

THE PRESENCE OF GOD IN HUMAN SUFFERING

Few places in the Old Testament reflect the participating Presence of God in the suffering of God's people more than do Jeremiah's writings. God says: "They have healed the wound of my people lightly, saying, 'Peace, peace,' when there is no peace" (6:14). Jeremiah himself takes up the spirit of God's Presence and says: "For the wound of the daughter of my people is my heart wounded, I mourn, and dismay has taken hold on me" (8:21).

In the historical incarnation of God in Jesus Christ, He told us that His continuing disclosure of His Presence would be in the Holy Spirit who would make intercession for us as we pray. Human suffering would be the arena of His Presence where we could see Him with full vision. In Matthew 25:31–46, in the scene of the Last Judgment, He tells us that we will see—or fail to see—His Presence in the hungry whom we feed, the thirsty to whom we give drink, the stranger whom we welcome, the naked whom we clothe, the sick and imprisoned whom we visit.

Martin Luther beheld clearly Jesus' revelation of Himself in the suffering of Frederick of Saxony, who fell desperately sick in September, 1519. He wrote him a letter and said: "When . . . I learned . . . that your Lordship has been afflicted with grave illness and that Christ has at the same time become ill in you . . . I cannot pretend that I do not hear the voice of Christ crying out from your Lordship's body and flesh saying: 'I am sick.' This is so because such evils as illness . . . are not borne by us who are Christians but by Christ himself, our Lord and Savior, in whom we live, even as Christ plainly testifies . . . when he says: 'Inasmuch as ye have done it unto one of the least of my brethren, ye have done it unto me.' " [3]

As pastoral counselors, you and I see human suffering in communities, families, and individuals. As Isaiah said: "The whole head is sick, and the whole heart faint. From the sole of the foot even to the head, there is no soundness in it, but bruises and sores and bleeding wounds; they are not pressed out, or bound up, or softened with oil" (Isaiah 1:5–6).

We come face to face with the Presence of God in these acute exigencies of human suffering. We ask Him *privately*, as Mark says the disciples did after they were unable to heal the epileptic boy: "Why could we not heal them?" His answer was and is: "This kind cannot be driven out by anything but prayer" (Mark 9:29).

It is heartening and a sustaining grace, therefore, to see books like Richard Foster's *Celebration of Discipline,* where prayer and fasting are taken seriously. It is even more encouraging to see the increasing practice of the Presence of God among pastoral counselors. The good Lord knows that we experience enough suffering to see His Presence when we have eyes to see Him.

The Presence of God:
The Lasting Center of
Pastoral Counseling

. . . when the fire blazes, the wood must burn; but only the fire remains. I have made cinders, ashes, dusts of forests; only the flame is eternal, only the flame is enduring, only the flame is absolute among the Change. Oh God, for something outside of me to last.

Thomas Wolfe [1]

Jesus Christ is the same yesterday and today and for ever.

Hebrews 13:8

2
The Presence of God: The Lasting Center of Pastoral Counseling

THE HUNGER FOR PERMANENCE IN THE FACE OF CHANGE

A persistent pang of hunger for most, if not all, human beings is for a relationship with another person or other persons that will last. The prayer of desperation of the human heart is for someone beyond the perimeters of our own selfhood whose love and acceptance will outlast us. Lurking within us is a test question for all those we know: "If I reveal myself to you as I really am, will you be able to take it, or will you abandon me? Will whatever there may be between us last?"

My purpose in this book is twofold: (1) To reflect briefly with you on the transient, temporary, unreliable centers of pastoral counseling; and (2) to explore with you the difference it can make if you and I make the Presence of the Eternal God the central dynamic in our dialogue with counselees. In essence, I want to move *from dialogue to trialogue* in pastoral counseling.

23

LASTING THINGS?

As you and I search for lasting metaphors to clothe such a goal with meaning, we can point to the prevalent American resistance to *repairing* things we own, such as a writing pen, a kitchen appliance, an automobile, and so on. Too often I have readily just "traded for" a new one. Then I say: "Maybe this one will last." I even take out insurance—that is, "buy a service contract"—to ward off the anxiety and expense associated with repairing the thing. But my fondest fantasy, upon my car's having broken down, is to take it back to the place where I got it and get a new replacement without cost to me. I suffer quite a blow to my self-esteem if the merchant finds in the broken object clear evidence that I have myself been misusing it. For example, my car doors must be closed, I learned upon the dealer's close inquiry, for the seat belts to work properly. I had been leaving a door ajar!

LASTING BODIES?

The need for that which lasts ceases to be a metaphor and becomes quite literal when we consider our own bodies. Manifestly, you do not "have" a body; you "are" a body. You and I live with the illusion that this body will last forever. Consequently, we tend to assume that we can do anything we choose with it without penalty. We can eat any way we like; we can drink to our own satisfaction; we can deny bodies of rest; we can drive automobiles or fly planes at any speed and without wearing seat belts. We do not confer with our bodies at any time to see how wear and tear are affecting them. Then, one day, our body enters a protest with *symptoms.* Damaged lungs, clogged liver, a biochemical depression, or body joints damaged by excess weight let us know that the body can be damaged and that it does not have a guarantee against its destruction. The body, too, may not last as long as it was created to last.

LASTING FRIENDSHIPS AND MARRIAGES?

I have noticed that a certain counselee of mine, who had consistently ignored his responsibility to other people by sexually "using" them, became more concerned about this after a close brush with cancer. There is the need for a relationship to last into the interpersonal sphere. Personal friendships stand or fall on the capacities of friends to form and maintain durable or lasting relationships.[2] Whether or not we admit it to ourselves, our personal friendships are haunted by a truly awful sense of impermanence. Children and youth, especially, suffer this in the face of the threat of nuclear war. Sales people on an airplane or at a sales convention, young adults being moved by their companies again and again, church members meeting in work and worship, old and infirm people in a nursing home, seminarians in a clinical pastoral education group—all these and more relate to each other furtively in the unspoken awareness that the friendships they form will "pass."

Friendships between men and women, men and men, and women and women easily become sexual. Hidden within a sexual relationship are many assumptions, conscious or unconscious, spoken or unspoken. Two assumptions emerge sooner or later, depending upon the ethical ability of the persons involved: First, the assumption that the partners are being sexual to the exclusion of "all others"; second, the sexual bond will be a permanent one. These categorical imperatives operate as unspoken assumptions whether the couple spells them out in a verbal covenant or not. I observe these assumptions in the thought and behavior of persons in considerably casual and nonchalant sexual liaisons.

Similarly, in both heterosexual and homosexual liaisons, a maxim can be stated: The more social approval, social reinforcement, and emotional support a couple receives and the more committed the couple is to making the relationship last indefinitely, the more likely the marriage is to last. Alfred Kinsey, the author of the massive study of American sexual behavior, said that he and his associates had examined over six thousand marital histories and three thousand divorce histories. They concluded that no one factor contributed to the durability of a marriage more than the simple determination to make the relationship persist.[3] The febrile anxiety of impermanence pervades even the most secure of friendships, liaisons, and marriages.

INTERMINABLE PASTORAL COUNSELING?

The pastoral counseling relationship itself is weighed in the balances on the scales of durability. Is this a one-time, for-the-time-being interview? Will these two people see each other again? How many times? Or, does it move on the tacit assumption that it will be a perpetual process? If this is to be an endless counseling relationship, what hazards do the counselor and counselee face in the decisions from time to time as to what they mean to each other? What place do they have in each other's lives? Also, what threats of hostility, withdrawal, apathy, manipulation, seduction, and so on emerge to break or end the relationship? Is "being counseled" a way of life for the counselee, or is it a temporary process with an agreed-upon end?

When and if the relationship fulfills its purposes, what new form do the continuing lives of counselor and counselee take? Do they have *other* more lasting identities with each other, such as teacher-student, worship leader and communicant, "friends of each other's family," or some other communal interaction? In other words, how do they handle the unspoken assumption that a pastor's relationship to those whom he or she serves has its roots in their common histories and its fruition in Eternity?

PERMANENCE—A CENTRAL VALUE?

These observations about the yearning for permanence in human relationships evoke the questions: "Granted that the lasting relationships are quantitative ones, how about the quality of the relationship? Is endurance the *central* concern of human beings?" When I buy a pair of shoes that do not fit, am I doomed to "wear them out"? Permanence for permanence's sake can be a destructive idolatry. Never had this become so vivid as when a counselee of mine said that he was hesitant to invest himself in the counseling process for fear that I would die! My comment was: "I, too, am mortal. Are you not so, also?" All human beings are mortal; pastors are human beings. Therefore, pastors are mortal! Mere durability evades this rather obvious but hard-to-accept fact. These realities uncover the idolatrous fantasy that any human relationship can be eternal, all-supplying, and never-denying.

Making the need for a lasting relationship *central* is hazardous to your and my health. It distorts and fouls out one relationship after another, and makes an absolute virtue of longevity of human life and personal relationships to others. Nevertheless, these distortions make all the more necessary the intensive search for the more durable relationship to the Eternal Presence of God for human relationships generally and for the pastoral counseling relationship in particular.

SHIFTING CENTERS OF PASTORAL COUNSELING

Historically, we pastoral counselors have devoted our lives to the careful, intentional, and scientifically informed relationship of the pastor to people in the clutch of perplexities. Consequently, we have found a wide range of qualitative centers for our working as pastoral counselors. These centers have at times expressed themselves in transient fads in much the same way as the Athenians and foreigners who "spent their time in nothing except telling or hearing something new" (Acts 17:21). Serious pastoral counselors have not been dilettantes such as these. To the contrary, first one group of pastoral counselors and then another have been more like frontier settlers. They have found a new territory that was imminently suited to their temperament, settled down in this or that approach to pastoral counseling. Then they made that approach the central heart of their interpretation of life for themselves and for those whom they counsel. Let me illustrate this.

PREACHING

Early in the emergence of the modern forms of pastoral counseling, Christian pastors in working churches developed their counseling ministry with preaching from the pulpit as its central focus. In Britain, the preaching of Leslie Weatherhead and his pastoral care of the congregation at City Temple in London became a role model for focusing the work of pastoral counseling around the center of a gifted preaching ministry.

In this country, the preaching of Harry Emerson Fosdick was measured by him as being effective in terms of the number of persons who sought personal counseling. John Sutherland Bonnell, in the same time frame, in addition to being a highly effective preacher, was intensely concerned with the confessional responsibility of the pastor in the context of preaching. Also, the positive-thinking preaching of Norman Vincent Peale eventuated in the establishment of the Marble Collegiate program in religion and psychotherapy.

Preaching has continued to be part and parcel of the pastoral counseling of many persons. The work of David McCleland in his interpretation of *pastoral* preaching, that of Charles Kemp in life-situation preaching, that of John Killinger in his person-centered preaching, and that of James Cox in his interpretation of biblical preaching, have sustained the integral relationship of pastoral counseling. However, because of intense shifts of emphasis and concern among pastoral counselors, preaching does not dominate the scene today as the controlling center of pastoral counseling.

VISITATION OF THE SICK

Coming into the arena concurrent in time with the heyday of "counseling preachers" was the work of Richard Cabot, Russell Dicks, and Anton Boisen. Cabot and Dicks shifted the focus of pastoral counseling from the congregation at worship to the medical and surgical hospital bedside ministry of the pastor. Anton Boisen shifted the center of the caring relationship to the hospital visit paid to a psychiatric patient. *Visitation,* not preaching, became the central focus.

I remember the first time that this shift of center occurred to me. I had spent six years in developing my preaching ministry as the pastor of churches. Then I became a chaplain in a general hospital. Late one afternoon, a nurse called me and said that a male patient on her ward wanted to see me.

I went immediately to his bedside. He greeted me with a direct question: "Be you the man of God in this hospital?" I had never been asked this question. I paused long enough to take two or three deep breaths. I straightened up my posture. I said: "Yes, sir, I am the man of God in this place!" He said: "Well, then, you know how the axe flew off the handle and landed in the creek and the man of God helped them to get it back." I remembered the dramatic story (which I later located in 2 Kings 6:7ff) of how Elisha had helped retrieve an axe head. He said: "Well, the axe has done flew off the handle for me. I've never been sick a day in my life, but now they tell me I got cancer of the bowels. They are gonna cut on me tomorrow. So I sent for you! Can you help me?"

Suddenly, I realized that neither he nor I was alone. God was with us. Though the body of this man was in jeopardy, the Eternal was his Sustainer. I was a messenger of that Presence in visitation.

ANALYTIC PSYCHOTHERAPY

However, within the context of the clinical pastoral education of ministers, a new center of concentration emerged in the work of Frederick Kuether, whose influence has not been adequately assessed or appreciated. He and a tight-knit group of like-minded persons were wholeheartedly fixed upon becoming psychoanalytically educated psychotherapists. A highly Americanized version of Freudian thinking and therapy became the heart, head, and hand of all that they did in pastoral counseling.[4]

This tradition is still an unquestioned commitment of a considerable number, although not all, of the members of the American Association of Pastoral Counselors. To have adequate credentials, from this point of view, a person must have been psychoanalyzed and must practice pastoral counseling as a form of psychoanalytic treatment. Even within the field of psychiatry as a medical specialty, considerable debate occurs as to whether the biochemical treatment of psychiatric patients has antiquated psychoanalytic methodology. Nevertheless, the sub-specialty of child psychiatry is heavily centered still in psychoanalysis. The fact that the psychoanalyst does not rely to much of an extent on the medication of patients still makes this a point of centering of pastoral counseling alluring to many pastoral counselors.

PASTORAL COUNSELING CENTERS

However, regardless of the ideological stance of pastoral counselors, vis-a-vis psychoanalysis, one major shift of a center for pastoral counseling occurred as a result of the Kuether tradition. The focus of attention moved away from bedside visitation, except for the basic training of clinical pastoral education, to the formal interview situation of office counseling. Churches have been very reluctant, if not apathetic or hostile, to "blessing" formal pastoral counseling as a funded and routine ministry of the church as a congregation. Token support is more often given to pastoral counseling centers.

Intensely active members of congregations tend not to use the services of a counseling service even in their own church building. They seem to prefer to seek out such care (a) from someone other than their parish pastor, (b) from someone who is a total stranger to them, their family, and their congregation, and (c) from someone whose religious convictions, nevertheless, are in keeping with their own. They even tend to choose a psychiatrist, who is always a medical doctor, in terms of his or her practice of a particular religious faith. Pastoral counseling centers, as a result of a confluence of these and many other forces, are becoming more and more available throughout the United States.

The centering of pastoral counseling has shifted dramatically from a Freudian or Sullivanian kind of psychoanalysis. The earliest shift was to the use of the client-centered therapy classically stated by Carl Rogers. The late 1950s, the 1960s, and even the early 1970s were "directed" by an allegiance to being "non-directive." As in the instance of psychoanalytic influences, so has the Rogerian been a controlling central commitment of a large number of pastoral counselors. Its lasting quality has been impressive, but not convincing. It, too, has begun to fade in behalf of the more realistic use of pastoral initiative and other more pastorally active kinds of pastoral approaches.

The Pop-Psychology "Cafeteria"

Nevertheless, pastoral counselors have moved on to first one and then the other psychotherapeutic "centerings" of their work. In the early 1970s, transactional analysis became a shorthand, Berlitz transformation of the enduring elements of psychoanalysis, shorn of some of its imperial dogmas about the fatedness of human nature. The analysis of the process of deception in the "gamesmanship" of American people has been chosen as *the* center of the work of the minister by a considerable number of pastoral counselors. Transcendental meditation, for other pastoral counselors, became the controlling motif of their counseling.

The rather gullible obeisance implicit to the Maharishi nullified much of this.

The more adequate influence of Henri Nouwen in a distinctly Christian approach to meditation has served to make TM's influence on pastoral counseling somewhat negligible. The more fully orbed findings of transpersonal psychologists have also eclipsed this influence. Time and space would fail me even to name the many other psychological foci pastoral counselors have centered upon, such as Gestalt psychology, "bipolar" approaches, psychosynthesis, and so on. At the present time, all of the periodic "centerings" of which mention has been made in this all too sketchy summary are under review (it seems to me). A serious reexamination of the spiritual life, and a reassessment of pastoral counseling in terms of our unique responsibility as spiritual directors of persons' faith development, is taking the center. Hence, I hope this book is a timely encouragement that the Presence of God be our central focus.

THE BIBLE

Even when a pastoral counselor decides, as I did in 1952, to be biblically centered in his or her search for a lasting center of pastoral counseling, he or she can easily become as doctrinaire and as ideologically off-center as psychoanalytic or Rogerian devotees. Taking the Bible as an end in itself and apart from the Presence of God to which it bears witness, the pastoral counselor misses the whole point of the Bible. The letter of the Bible can kill; the Spirit gives life.

Apart from having my eyes opened to the Scriptures, as happened to the two persons on the road to Emmaus, the Bible itself is no adequate center for pastoral counseling. It can be a law book for my pridefully becoming a "judge and divider" over people's human affairs. Jesus Himself refused this fate (Luke 12, 13ff). In the face of such contention, Jesus saw the shortness of life, the transience of inheritances, and the certainty of death. The Bible can be used as a law book in such cases. The pride, self-elevation, greed, and power-hungriness of people will simply find biblical justification. In pastoral counseling, wherever I have seen the Bible used as the very center of the process, invariably, the problem being considered—divorce, remarriage, Christians suing each other in court, and so on—ceases to be the issue. The main issue becomes the *infallibility* of the interpretation being given. And our eyes are closed to this.

Something else *must* be the lasting center. Then all these others will fall into place.

Therefore, the purpose of this book is to explore the guiding accounts of the epiphanies and theophanies describing the Presence of God in living conversation with persons and to interpret the pastoral counseling relationship with the Presence of God as its lasting and abiding center. My hope is that this reality can be to the pastoral counselor a "cloud by day and a pillar of fire by night" in the wildernesses of the human spirit in which we journey with our counselees.

In this the fortieth year of my career as a pastoral counselor, I have found my concern for the Presence of God in a trialogue with counselees to be the living heart of my work. For me, this is no intellectual formulation neglecting the responsiveness so vital to a pastoral counselor. Nor is the Presence of God a constant awareness of mine.

As Samuel Terrien says: "The reality of the presence of God stands at the center of Biblical faith. This presence, however, is always elusive. 'Verily, verily, thou art a God that hidest thyself.' " 5

God's Presence does not keep a therapeutic schedule at the beck and call of a pastoral counselor. God surprises both counselor and counselee with joy, understanding, and awe. Often God prepares us for the mystic vision of His glory through the hungering darkness of our awareness of the absence of God. Martin Marty has demonstrated this vividly in his profound study, *The Cry of Absence.* Yet, the pastoral counselor who accepts the quest for the Presence of God as the central focus of his or her counseling will have a *lasting* center, one that lives on past the threat of condemnation, the threat of meaninglessness, and the threat of aging and death.

I have not come to this realization in a momentary enthusiasm nor out of a desire to seem more or less pious than I am. Over the years, my most significant memories in pastoral counseling have been in those spiritual breakthroughs when the Presence of God became intensely evident without contrivance or technique on my part and much to the awe-struck amazement on both the counselee's and my part. An Eternal "centering" happens. As Thomas Merton says, the relationship "is centered entirely on attention to the presence of God and to His will and His love." [6]

Cognitively, I have groped after this center for what we do as pastoral counselors. I have found "way stations" along the course of my pastoral pilgrimage. I have written down descriptions of these "way stations" from time to time. The most continuous record is found in the 1951, 1964, and 1982 editions of my book, *The Christian Pastor.* In the first edition, I centered pastoral care and counseling in the pastor's representation of God's Presence at times of crisis. In the second edition, I focused our work on the identity and integrity of the pastor as a "teacher come from God." In the 1982 edition, I concentrated on the pastor's participation in the wisdom or counsel of God in the exercise of the gift of discernment. The pastor is a *tebunah,* a person of understanding (Proverbs 20:5).

In other works I have been more systematically oriented in my effort to "unskew" the pastoral counseling relation from a temporary and unstable center. In my book, *Religious Factors in Mental Illness,* I emphasized idolatry as the distinctly religious factor in mental illness. In *Protestant Pastoral Counseling,* written eight years later, I developed this idea positively in relating pastoral counseling to the Protestant principle of resistance to any absolutizing of relative entities, such as the infallibility of any church or psychotherapeutic system. In a chapter on the Holy Spirit as Counselor, you will find the earliest formulation I have made on the theme of this book. In fact, this book is a "twenty-one-years-later" sequel to that book, now out of print. I hope you will be able to find a copy of it in your local library or through a secondhand book agency. Instead of trying to rewrite and update it, I have chosen to write a new book instead.

All along the way, I have kept technically informed about various schools of psychotherapy to which I have referred as options for centering pastoral counseling chosen by fellow pastoral counselors. The primary sources of psychoanalysis, individual psychology, the interpersonal psychiatry of Sullivan, client-centered therapy, transactional analysis, clinical psychiatry, cognitive therapy, and biochemical therapy have enriched my counseling.

I have worked in clinical situations alongside highly competent clinicians who have mastered the skills in each of these kinds of therapy. My purpose in doing this has been to be informed by, without being centered upon, any one of these therapeutic disciplines.

I do not perceive myself as being an "eclectic" pastoral counselor. My own theological belief center has and will continue to separate me from any ideological polarization into a psychotherapeutic mold. To me, only an explicit and articulate concern for the appearing of the Presence of God in the pastoral counseling relationship is an adequate centering of pastoral counseling. The two great commandments of the wholehearted love of God and neighbor provide a base of operations large enough to enable you and me to learn from any one or all systems of therapy without being imperialized by any one or more of them. God has made none of these common or unclean. God may reveal His Presence through any of them, even when a particular theorist may "know it not."

The Presence of God
As Creator

I ask no dream, no prophetic ecstasies
No sudden rending of the veil of clay
No angel visitant, no opening skies;
But take the dimness of my soul away.

George Croly (1780–1860)

3
The Presence of God
As Creator

The very thought of the Presence of God in the process going on between us and our counselees tends to suggest immediately that you, I, and our counselees must enter a mystical and even ecstatic experience. Yet, the task of pastoral counseling is often everything but that! In its "day-to-dayness," pastoral counseling only rarely reaches such heights of the spiritual life. More often, it consists of trudging with the counselee through seemingly endless detail to find an occasional treasure of simple wisdom.

Pastoral counseling does become dramatic in that it is ordinarily prompted and begun by a severe crisis in people's lives. A measure of desperation creates the need for a counselor. Even so, one person's crisis is often an everyday occurrence to another. Even the crises have a certain predictable routineness about them. The hazard of becoming "hardened" to them must be resisted by a caring pastoral counselor.

What, to us, may be a repetitive event may be a once-in-a-lifetime event for the counselee. When we take a "ho-hum" inner posture of spirit, we soon become transparent to a desperate person. We have too much realism and common sense to expect pastoral counseling to be a perpetual Mount of Transfiguration. Nevertheless, we can ask that God take such dimness of our souls away. The Eternal does indeed become known in the ordinary.

The Presence of God can indeed be perceived by you and me without "prophetic ecstasies" and "sudden rendings." The apostle Paul gives us the working hypothesis we need for discerning the Presence of God in pastoral counseling on a day-by-day basis. In Romans 1:19ff, he says: "For what can be known about God is plain to them, because God has shown it to them. Ever since the creation of the world his invisible nature, namely his eternal power and deity, has been clearly perceived in the things that have been made." He points to the plainly perceivable Presence of God in creation, i.e., the focus of our discussion in this chapter. You and I do not have to be hermits, clairvoyants, or spiritual athletes in meditation to perceive the Presence of God. God lets us know plainly in creation.

The Image of God in Counselee and Counselor

You and I *perceive* the person, the couple, the family, or the group with whom we counsel from some particular angle of vision at all times. As it really happens, we perceive them differently from varied depths of our being. Bringing these different perceptions into a unified vision is both a calling and a discipline. For example, we may perceive this person from the data they give us about their station in life—their age, sex, marital status, parental status, educational level, vocational situation, and so on. In addition, we may perceive them in terms of their particular "problem" which they unfold before us. We may perceive them in terms of a diagnostic system, a system of ethical and spiritual development, or a theological assumption as to whether they are in or out of a community of faith.

More subtly and personally than the objective appraisals, we have a set of internal communications going on within us. In spite of their private nature, these inner musings are quite conscious to us. For example, we feel comfortable in their presence, or they bother us. We are "drawn" to them, or they repel us. We are interested in them, or they bore us. We basically like them, dislike them, or they leave us "cold." They remind us of this person, that person, or the other person whom we have met before. All of these have much to do with our perception of them as persons. As we shall see in the next chapter, they may be uncannily *strange* to us.

Even more profoundly than all of these, we have a more or less unconscious set of values and assumptions about our own lives and those of others. We "price" the person or persons sitting before us. We may value them in terms of their prestige in the community, because we are in search of prestige. We may value them in terms of our own assumptions of beauty and ugliness in human beings. We may value them in terms of whether they "belong" to our particular belief community as expressed in such things as a "genuinely intellectual" person, a psychologically sophisticated person, a true believer, a radical, a "redneck," or a "far out" person. These are price tags we place upon them, wittingly or not.

In the face of such estimates, classical Christian faith starts with the assumption that any person is created in the image of God. If we are intent upon realizing the Presence of God in creation, we purpose to reach behind all other perceptions of this person or these persons to value them primarily as persons made in the image of God. As Emil Brunner says: "We would do well to understand 'image' in the sense of reflection, that is, an existence which points back or refers back to something else." [1] The very presence of this other person, this family of persons, or this group of persons points back or refers back to the Presence of God. They are persons made in the image of God. We do not worship them or allow them to worship us. We point away from ourselves and toward God. Their worth and our worth do not reside in ourselves, "but in the One who stands over against (us), in Christ, the Primal Image, and in the Word of God." [2] Our value is a derived one by reason of God, who created us. This takes all other "price tags" from our perceptions and becomes our royal road to the Presence of God in the being of our counselee(s). If indeed you and I have any counsel to offer, it comes from the very image of God in us, as well. Such a perception of our relationship to our counselee brings the meeting of selves to worshipful heights of devotional and ethical responsibility.

THE IMAGE OF GOD: PROMPTER TO PRAYER

In this sense, pastoral counseling itself becomes prayer. We ask God to open our eyes and unseal our ears that we may discern God's image in the faces and in the utterances of those whom we counsel. Counselees can defy our every effort to enlist them in an alliance that moves away from the destructiveness of their past sufferings and toward a new beginning in their lives. They "dig their heels in" and commit themselves to helplessness. This renders the counselor powerless. You can easily throw up your hands. You can lose patience. Or, you can look past their fretful ragings. You can wait patiently for their basic dignity as a person made in the image of God to come forward. You wait.

You pray that you may not weary of them. You are gripped by your own finiteness, your own weariness. You shift into a quiet listening, as far as the counselee can see. It is an intense, petitioning kind of prayer before God, from your standpoint. You wait upon the Lord that both your and the counselee's strength may be renewed. You ask that energy and hope will be provided for the time at hand and until you see them again. You ask for patience that your own frustration will not curdle what good will God has already given you into hostility and pious instructions against this person before you. In that event, they probably will have already heard from others what you would have to say. Our personal devotions, as we contemplate the image of God in those to whom we minister, become ethical enquiry rooms of our own hearts.

THE IMAGE OF GOD: ETHICAL CATALYST

Ethical issues arise in the stewardship of the hostility counselees engender within us. Similarly, the flattery, gifts, and erotic seductions of counselees obscure the image of God in them from themselves and from us. Counseling with "very important persons"—VIPs—may blandish us away from the search for the very image of God within them. The seductions of power handily outdistance the allures of sexuality. In fact, the sexual overtures of persons may be facades for their greed for prestige, a place in the public eye, and control over other people with whom they are competing. All the while, the too easily seduced pastoral counselor may be thinking it is his or her irresistible sexual charms!

A conscious intention to seek the Presence of the image of God within the seductive counselee transcends the purely horizontal interpretation of the relationship as a "transference" and "counter-transference." What psychoanalysis teaches us about this phenomenon of the "family romance" of sexuality is not to be discounted but used assiduously. Ordinarily, it is used sloppily in pastoral counseling and psychiatric case conferences and supervision. The sibling rivalry and power politics involved in such assessments are often too close to home to get much attention. These aspects of transference and counter-transference are displaced to the more titillating sexual issues, often at the expense of females in the dramas being discussed. Once again, the power dimensions of the Temptation story get neglected in deference to the male-female equation or lack of equation. Greed for power is glossed over with accusations of concupiscence.

The ethical concerns in male-female interaction in pastoral counseling are, nevertheless, focused by the intentional search for the image of God in both male and female. Carl Jung insists upon our considering the balanced presence of both the male and female principle in every person. When as a Christian we do this, it points us toward the Presence of God, unifying harmoniously these two principles to match the physiology of the bodies we have been given at conception and birth. As Emil Brunner says again: "A human being is individualized just as much by the fact of being male or female as by the fact that he or she belongs to a particular race, or by his or her intellectual endowments." [3] In both creation and redemption, the dependence and submission of the sexes is a *mutual* and not a one-way submission of men and women to each other. It is only in the fallen and broken state of sin that they arrogate themselves over each other. The ethical issues involved in this relationship are the stuff of which marriage and family therapy (as done by a pastoral counselor) are made. We rightly seek the full expression of the image of God in a husband-wife relationship. We do so by insisting on a *just* covenant between them as the fountain of trust and respect that nurtures the unambivalent love of mature marriage.

Similarly, when pastoral counselors meet the issue of homosexuality in a counseling situation, sooner or later the question is raised or an assertion made to the effect that "God made me like this." Is this true? The question is not whether this person is a greater sinner than others, as many self-righteous would say. The question is rather: "Is homosexuality inherent in the image of God, or does it in its own particular way exclude the other side of the human race in its sexuality?" I think it does, and that this is *not* the way God makes us. People learn this from someone else, not God.

Let us return to the problem of transference love in the pastoral counseling relationship for another ethical issue catalyzed by experiencing the Presence of God in God's image in ourselves and our counselees. When writing on the clinical problem of sexual love between patient and physician, Sigmund Freud spoke clearly: "For the doctor, ethical motives unite with the technical ones to restrain him from giving the patient his love. . . . it is quite out of the question for the analyst to give way. However highly he may prize love he must prize even more highly the opportunity for helping his patient over a decisive stage in her life. She has to learn from him to overcome the pleasure principle, to give up a satisfaction which lies to hand but is socially not acceptable, in favour of a more distant one, which is perhaps altogether uncertain, but which is both psychologically and socially unimpeachable." [4] This comment from Freud stands in stark contrast to the codelessness of many therapists today at the strictly humanistic level. The pastoral counselor, by profession and ordination, meets the image of God in the person of the opposite sex toward whom he or she is sexually attracted.

To do less than Freud insists is not only to be liable to professional malpractice claims. It is also to deface the image of God in that person and in oneself. The devotional imperative is to counsel the widowed and orphaned and to keep oneself with clean hands and a reasonably pure heart in the process. This is pure religion and undefiled before God (James 1:27). It makes for an ethically dependable and genuinely reverent pastoral counselor. James 1:27 seems to be built upon Psalm 24:3–5. These verses have been a guide for me in my care of deprived, lonely, and vulnerable people.

INTERPERSONAL CHAOS AND THE PRESENCE OF GOD

"The earth was without form and void, and darkness was upon the face of the deep; and the Spirit of God was moving over the face of the waters." The formlessness and emptiness of chaos in the face of the deep at the outset of God's creation of the earth symbolizes, for me, the interpersonal chaos people bring to a first pastoral counseling interview. If I did not believe that it is God and not I, the Spirit of God and not mine, that is moving upon the face of the depths of the tense and disordered lives, I would take up a more tangible and easily managed task than pastoral counseling. Two dramatic situations presented themselves to me this past week. They illustrate this chaos and the yearning for order and peace.

A couple came in desperation over their inability to find any semblance of order in their chaotic marriage and parenting situation. They themselves as husband and wife and their children from three different marriages were involved. They painfully introduced me to the complicated transactions going on between themselves and the five children, who ranged in ages from two to eighteen years of age. They told me of the stress and strain of coping with spouses from previous marriages. Wave after wave of confusion came from them to me, prompting me to ask myself: "Where do I take hold of this?" Later, as I meditated in my prayers, I asked: *"O God, where are You in their plight?"* One of them, toward the end of the interview, spoke of having prayed for the ability to get rid of anger and hatred. The chaos had evoked a prayer of desperation. Chaos seems to have the creative ability—to evoke prayer, that is. In a neurological metaphor, it has "evoke potential." This was the beginning of the answer to my quest for the Presence of God in this counseling situation.

The next day after I saw the couple just mentioned, I was called for a pastoral consultation on a psychiatric in-patient ward. I went to see a twenty-four-year-old man who, a year and a half ago, had suffered a head injury in an accident. It impaired his speech, his memory of words and their meaning, and his ability to concentrate for any long period of time. He became acutely depressed because he could not work. Confusion rules in his home. His father has been divorced and remarried three times, and his mother twice. He feels displaced in this situation.

He has begun to have intense clairvoyant feelings that he can foretell events which will happen. He is also very religious and has gotten the distinct leading from God that a great change—the exact nature of which he does not know—is about to take place. He feels that he must have every minute detail of his life in order, such as his insurance policies, his last will and testament, and all of his personal farewells, because he does not have any idea what will happen to him. His family assumed that he was going to commit suicide and therefore had him hospitalized. He insists that he does not plan to kill himself. To the contrary, he is going to destroy the gun collection he has so that no one can use them to kill, because he is a devout Christian opposed to war.

Everything must be put in order. He vaguely associates his system of thought with the possibility of a "new age," and even more vaguely, to the immediate return of our Lord Jesus Christ. This man is overwhelmed by the chaos in his life. A highly competent team of physicians, nurses, and social workers are my colleagues who carry the major responsibility for his well-being. Our assignment by the Eternal is to join Him as He moves over the turbulent chaos of this man's life and that of his family and friends.

The man puts into words, however occult in their meaning, his need for order. He searches for an overview of the interacting systems of the continuing creative work of God. Theological "over-againstness" with such a disciplined scientific team is as unnecessary as it is unproductive. The work of the neurosurgeons and neurologists who saved the man's life entered the biosphere of his being at one level of the system of his growing life. The psychiatrists enter at another level, the biochemical and lingual and interpersonal system of his being. The social workers involve the family system, of which the man is a part, and mobilize the vocational and educational forces of the community in this man's behalf. The parish pastor relates the community of the people of God to him. They sustain a strong life-support system for both the man and his family.

Whether anyone is *aware* of the Presence of God does not determine whether God *is* of *is not* moving as Creator over the face of this intricate, hurting, disordered, chaotic system. God pays little or no attention to my and the rest of the therapeutic team's neat role distinctions, demarcations of sacred and secular, or hierarchies of scientific and/or religious knowledge. This Creator, God, says that the first shall be last, the last shall be first. Nothing He has created is common or unclean. If we receive anything God has made with prayer and thanksgiving, it is consecrated. The whole earth is full of His glory. That glory comes ever so silently, and the Presence of God becomes inarticulately real when the artificial walls of separation (that might exist between staff members) disappear. A koinonia of celebration will come when this patient becomes free of despair and enters into a creative function himself, in spite of the injury he has sustained.

CREATION AND PROVIDENCE IN HUMAN GROWTH

Henry Van Dyke's hymn says:

> Joyful, joyful we adore Thee,
>   God of glory, Lord of love;
> Hearts unfold like flowers before Thee,
>   opening to the sun above. . . .

Not only hearts unfold, but human lives as a whole unfold in well-provided-for growth and development. When we follow the course of the conception, gestation, and birth of a child, we are astounded that the overwhelmingly large percentage of children are born healthy and well-formed. Our awesome sense of the Providence of God in creating life continues as we see predictable phases in the child's personality and social development take place with a wisdom working from within the child "bringing up each individual child in his or her own particular way, so that he or she becomes an adult they may be themselves." The Creator stages the phasing of human development that takes place. Providence is God's gracious outworking of His purposes in creation and culminating His redemption in the fullness of a person's mature relationship to Christ in salvation. Our studies of the development of personality are empirical ways of providing rough charts of this development. If we look at Providence as "seeing ahead," such charting of the development of large numbers and populations of people is an effort to anticipate and to predict "the shape of things to come" in people's lives.

The pastoral counselor discerns the Presence of God as One by whose Providence people's lives follow a discernible pattern of growth by which both he or she and those with whom they counsel can be alerted, comforted, and warned about the possible outcomes of their lives. One does not need to be clairvoyant to be able to know that the thirty-year-old son or daughter of a seventy-year-old parent, who is still slavishly dependent upon the parent, will face a major disaster if and when that parent dies. The retarded emotional and social maturity of the son or daughter has in it its own built-in tragedy. This is reminiscent of the comment of the distinguished psychoanalyst, Karen Horney, who said: "Life itself is the great therapist; it is the only therapist who does not ask whether the patient can take the treatment!" Seen from the perspective of both the goodness and severity of God, the discernible and predictable process of personality development and historical events in government and nations are visible manifestations of both the kindness and the severity of God (Romans 11:22). God neither tinkers with His creation nor leaves those who do unaccountable for having done so.

IDOLATRY AND THE PRESENCE OF GOD IN CREATION

The apostle Paul penetrates the confusion in our minds as to the Presence of God in creation, after having said that "ever since the creation of the world his invisible nature . . . has been clearly perceived in the things that have been made." Then he says that persons who claim to be wise have become fools; ". . . they exchanged the truth about God for a lie and worshiped and served the creature rather than the Creator . . ." (Romans 1:20, 25). In other words, they became idolators of creatures instead of worshipers of God, the Creator.

The word "exchanged" has an interesting metaphor from modern business. In the marketplace of life, it would be diverting money, commodities, or energy away from its original purpose. In moral theology, it would mean perversion. The original purpose of people is to "worship God and enjoy Him forever," says the Westminster Catechism. To divert or pervert one's purpose from this is idolatry. When this happens, you or I invest a finite, temporary, perishing part of creation with infinite, permanent, and eternal qualities. That object of adoration or desecration, love or hate, begins and continues to possess us. We are obsessed with and possessed by it. It becomes the center of our existence. We have, as Milton said, "given our lives away, a sordid boon." The demonic distortions, or "off-centerings," we observe in pastoral counseling and self-examination take over. This is the plain meaning of the Scripture about demonic possession that "deliverance counselors" and exorcists do not often mention. Several examples from both the New Testament and from clinical pastoral practice may be cited.

Both the New Testament and psychoanalysis insist that in the process of maturity a person leave his or her father and mother for a mission in the larger family of the human race. Also, to form a love relationship to a member of the opposite sex in marriage, a person must leave father and mother and cleave to that mate. Not to do this results in a fixation upon one or the other, or both, parents that distorts and inhibits a person's growth.

The major difference between the teachings of Jesus and psychoanalysis is that the latter dwells on the fixation and looks to the individual to use the insight to manage his or her life better by a courageous act of will. The New Testament, to the contrary, says that "in the beginning it was not so," i.e., the Creator intended that a person leave father and mother. He or she is empowered to do so by reason of the larger love of God and neighbor.

The New Testament, especially in Jesus' teachings, points away from the idolatry of parents to the rightful center of their worship. I like the wisdom of Anton Boisen when, on one occasion, he said that Freud insisted that the "God-concept" came from one's relationship to one's parents, when in reality it came from the individual's prior creation in the image of God. Parents, for their own reasons, diverted the child's worship of God from God to themselves. They actually are Promethean stealers of fire from heaven.

Pastoral counselors spend a considerable amount of time listening to counselees "speak evil of fathers and mothers." I have had far more than a mere apprentice discipline at this task. Enabling people to affirm what is good in their parents, that is, to honor their parents for the positive strengths they have received from them, and at the same time to forgive them for their blunders and malices, is a trek toward maturity with the counselee. Love is the force that overcomes the ambivalence we feel toward another; and maturity, in one sense, is coming to the point that we can forgive our parents for what we have against them.

In a more humorous vein, maturing means doing what you know is the right thing to do even if your parents suggested it! The acceptance of them as finite, limited, and sinful creatures in need of redemption from idolatry along with us is the best way to reach that maturity.

Finding our Creator as the true Center of our lives puts everyone and everything else in their rightful place, undistorted and serene, in our lives. We do not even have to spend our lives desecrating an idol who has let us down or contending with someone who demands absolute obeisance from us. We can just "let them *be.*" We do not have to wait around until our parents are buried. We can get on with our calling from the Lord Jesus right now. However, greed for money and property in a hoped-for inheritance can defer launching out on missions for the Lord Jesus Christ. Waiting to bury one's parents *may* be waiting for the inheritance!

The institution of marriage, and parenthood itself, can become an idolatrous construction diverting a counselor or counselee from the centered worship of the Creator. Jesus' comment that in the resurrection there will be neither marriage nor giving in marriage is a saying that is relevant to Paul's comment about exchanging the worship of the Creator for the worship of the creature.

I recall conversing with a woman whose grief over her divorce had so overwhelmed her that she had to be hospitalized. In one interview I said to her that possibly she had idolized her husband and that his rejection of her had shaken her faith. On the next interview she came back to this comment and said: "I think you are wrong. I do not idolize my husband. He is far too cruel for that. But I *do* idolize *being married.* I have been raised to feel that I do not exist unless I am married."

The unreality of this distortion and perversion of worship was the beginning of her patient journey back to health. Before the Creator, the true Center of her life, she learned that she had an identity of her own that preceded and outlasted the institution of marriage. Christ set her free from this kind of bondage. Patiently weaning a person from this bondage is what much pastoral counseling aims to do.

Closely related to the idolatry of parents and of the institution of marriage is the organization of one's whole life around the family fortune or inheritance. This is explicitly evident in the problems of the Prodigal Son described in Luke 15:11–24. He asked his father: "Father, give me the share of property that falls to me." The redeeming feature of his request was that he was forthright about it and was willing to settle the matter once and for all then, rather than wait around for his father to die. The centering of life around a family fortune is implicit in the story of the rich man in Luke 18:18–30, although only tradition suggests to us that he was a *young* person. Nevertheless, the wealth the man had was a central concern of his.

The focus on family wealth has been called an "inheritance complex" by Edmund Bergler several years ago in a book of his entitled *Money and Neurosis.* He dubs the process of centering one's life on money "a shifted omnipotence." He says that it is handed down from generation to generation in families. Money and property need not be this way, but they easily become so.

Time and space would fail us to enumerate all the idolatrous constructions with which we deal daily as pastoral counselors. Old grudges, competitive rat races in business and professional life, functional roles in life, addictive behaviors in substance abuse, religiosity, sexuality, food, work, and so on, become ruling obsessions. As John Calvin says: "The human mind is a perpetual forge of idols. . . . That idolatry has its origin in the idea which men have that God is not present unless his presence is carnally exhibited." [5]

A major contribution of Paul Tillich was his precise statement of the "Protestant Principle" in his assessment of both personal life and national pride as it appeared in the rise of Hitler's Third Reich. He defined the Protestant Principle as the protest against anything relative receiving absolute devotion which is to be given only to God. When we absolutize the relative, the demonic enters human relationships. Such foundations must of their own selves be shaken. As Hebrews 12:26–27 says: "His voice then shook the earth; but now he has promised, 'Yet once more I will shake not only the earth but also the heaven.' This phrase, 'Yet once more,' indicates the removal of what is shaken, as of what has been made, in order that what cannot be shaken may remain."

This shaking of the foundations of people's lives happens before the eyes of a pastoral counselor. Weather-beaten wisdom in pastoral counseling teaches us that some situations must get much worse before they can get better. Others avoid this fate until life itself shakes a self-destructive idolatry to pieces. Then, as Eric Berne puts it, the deadly games of life come into play, ending in divorce, surgery, or at the morgue. The Presence of God becomes apparent in the tragedies of idolatry. We really *shall* have no other gods before Him. Our very idolatries call painful attention to the Presence of the Eternal. In His creation, He has made us for Himself and our hearts are restless, chaotic, and idolatrous until we are centered in His loving Presence.

As Paul said to the Athenians at the Areopagus: "And he made from one every nation of men to live on all the face of the earth, having determined allotted periods and the boundaries of their habitation, that they should seek God, in the hope that they might feel after him and find him. Yet he is not far from each one of us, for 'In him we live and move and have our being'; as even some of your poets have said, 'For we are indeed his offspring' " (Acts 17:26–28).

The Presence of God in the Strange and the Stranger

Then Jacob awoke from his sleep and said: "Surely the Lord is in this place; and I did not know it." And he was afraid, and said, "How awesome is this place! This is none other than the house of God, and this is the gate of heaven."

Genesis 28:16–17

. . . I was a stranger and you welcomed me. . . .

Matthew 25:35b

Do not neglect to show hospitality to strangers, for thereby some have entertained angels unawares.

Hebrews 13:2

4
The Presence of God in the Strange and the Stranger

Marketplace thought about the Presence of God is one of sentimental familiarity. Country-western songs speak of "having a little talk with Jesus" almost as if the Lord were a chum with whom one has a chitchat. Even Tennyson speaks of the Presence of God as being "closer to us than breathing and nearer than hands and feet."

In stark contrast, however, is the persistent biblical wisdom that God's Presence comes to us when we know it not. At the least, our awareness of the Presence is an afterthought. At the most, God comes to us as a Stranger amid strange and foreign events. We are more or less ambushed by God's Presence in unexpected ways and unforeseen events. Serendipity characterizes God's ways of meeting us in the strange and in the stranger. As John Wesley said, we are "strangely warmed" by God's unexpected visitation.

Having worked for eleven years in a strange role for a minister (i.e., as a professor of psychiatry and behavioral sciences in a "secular" university), I find few perceptions of God's Presence more accurate than this—the strange and the stranger who becomes intensely evident when we least expect Him to do so. No easy contrivance can "incant" His Presence by some familiar spirit. No striking of an ecclesiastical posture reveals Him in such an environment. However, a spirit of welcome, hospitality, and anticipation at the appearance of the strange and the stranger is the discipline required in both the Old and New Testaments. The pastoral counselor's evenly hovering attentiveness to the strange and the stranger, with a capacity for awesome reverence for the unknown, is his or her invitation to and invocation of the Presence of God.

BIBLICAL AND CLINICAL COALESCENCES

THE NEED TO BE A PARENT

God appeared to Abraham in the three strange men (Genesis 18:1–16) at the oaks of Mamre. He graciously had water brought to wash their feet, invited them to rest under the tree, and provided them with food. They asked: "Where is Sarah, your wife?" In much the same way Jesus asked of the woman at the well that she bring her husband to Him. It is remarkable how God affirms His creative intention by persistently involving the marital partner of those with whom He deals. In this context, the Lord's message comes to Abraham and Sarah: "I will surely return to you in the spring, and your wife will have a son." The strangers were harbingers of God's good news.

The situation of the barren, infertile couple who come to a pastor is one of desperation. Today, the solace of the possibility of adopting a child is a vain hope because fewer mothers of unborn babies are willing to carry them to term. Those who do so less often give up their babies for adoption. The incapacity to have a child, therefore, becomes the occasion for a perpetual sorrow for many couples.

The dramatic results of artificial insemination and *in vitro* fertilization have made parenthood possible for some couples. In such instances, an awesome sense of the Holy pervades the sequestered conferences of medical teams, the pastoral consultant, and the expectant couple, even when no formal religiosity is evident.

Even more uncanny is the pastoral counseling situation in which one emotional impediment after another is replaced by a serene and relaxed relation of a couple's interaction with each other, and their worry is either overcome or removed. Then, when the "nest has been prepared," as one woman gynecologist described it, the miracle of conception occurs. Even the most secularized spirit is likely to say: "Thank God!" The spiritually disciplined are likely to say: "Surely the Lord is in this place; and I did not know it." Everybody enters an ecstatic aura of grace that no effortful striving could have precipitated.

PRESENCE, ESTRANGEMENT, AND DREAMS

Jacob cleverly purloined the birthright from his brother. As a result, he had to flee from the safe confines of his father's house. He had stepped out into strange territory without a light to help him tread safely into the unknown. Paul Tournier has aptly described the rhythm of spiritual growth as quitting one place and seeking a new place.[1] Jacob was doing just this. The anxiety and dread of the "betweenness" state is a time of strangeness. God came to him in a dream as he slept. God reassured him of His Presence with him. He promised him the land on which he was lying and said: "Behold, I am with you and will keep you wherever you go, and will bring you back to this land; for I will not leave you until I have done that of which I have spoken to you." When he awoke from his sleep, Jacob said: "Surely the Lord is in this place; and I did not know it" (Genesis 28:15, 16).

Here God does not come to Jacob as a stranger, but in a strange way. He comes in the strangeness of dreams. It took a hyperrationalistic theological world a long time to re-evaluate the role of dreams in revelation. However, dreams play a vital role in the drama of creation, redemption, and release of the human spirit in relation to God. God came to Abimelech in a dream and caused him to know that Sarah was Abraham's wife and not his sister, as he had said.

Joseph's dreams of his relationship to his parents and siblings provided him with the schema of his whole life story. Dreams and their interpretation became his royal road to the knowledge of God in his sojourn as a stranger in Egypt. His brothers derided him as a "master of dreams."

The life story of Daniel interpreted Nebuchadnezzar's dreams. God revealed the mystery of Nebuchadnezzar's dream to Daniel in a "vision of the night." For this gift of wisdom, Daniel blessed the God of heaven and said: "Blessed be the name of God for ever and ever, to whom belong wisdom and might. He changes times and seasons; he removes kings and sets up kings; he gives wisdom to the wise and knowledge to those who have understanding; he reveals deep and mysterious things; he knows what is in the darkness, and the light dwells with him. To thee, O God of my fathers, I give thanks and praise, for thou hast given me wisdom and strength, and hast now made known to me what we asked of thee, for thou hast made known to us the king's matter" (Daniel 2:20–23).

This is a remarkable response of a counselor's thanksgiving for wisdom and strength to do his work. We have learned much wisdom from the behavioral scientists about the nature of sleep, the psychology of dreams, and the psychotherapeutic utilization of dreams. We need not take as "gospel" their philosophical presuppositions and dogmas to gain wisdom from their precise, factual observations of dream behavior in patients. More likely than this is our pastoral neglect of the Presence of God in our own dream life and that of our counselees. I have repeatedly been astonished at the way in which a dream encounter with God has become the pattern for the whole spiritual direction of counselees who have come to me. In turn, my own dream life about my own personal spiritual pilgrimage has put me in touch with the Living Presence of God and given me concrete ethical guidance in my counseling with people who seek my help. Albert Meiburg, an esteemed colleague and friend, early demonstrated the integral role of dreams in the revelation of God as they are recorded in both the Old and the New Testaments.

In fact, both counselor and counselee in our waking hours sufficiently insulate ourselves from the Presence of God that if He does appear unto us, He has to catch us when we are asleep to do so!

THE PRESENCE OF GOD IN FAMILY CONFLICT

Jacob had stolen the birthright from his brother, and, aided and abetted by his mother, Rebekah, triangulated with his unseeing and aging father, Isaac. He fled at his father's and mother's behest to Paddan-aram, there to find wives with whom he parented children. Together they all prospered until the time came that he should return to the country of Esau, his brother, in the land of Seir, the country of Edom. As he drew near, he prayed: "O God of my father Abraham and God of my father Isaac, O Lord who didst say to me, 'Return to your country and to your kindred, and I will do you good,' I am not worthy of the least of all the steadfast love and all the faithfulness which thou hast shown to thy servant, for with only my staff I crossed this Jordan; and now I have become two companies. Deliver me, I pray thee, from the hand of my brother, from the hand of Esau, for I fear him, lest he come and slay us all, the mothers with the children. But thou didst say, 'I will do you good, and make your descendants as the sand of the sea, which cannot be numbered for multitude' " (Genesis 32:9–12).

Jacob prepared an impressive gift for his brother and sent it ahead of him. He and his family crossed the river Jabbok, and he sent them on ahead of him. He was left alone. In his solitude, he met a man who wrestled with him until the break of day. Jacob was a worthy opponent, but he sustained a thigh out of joint in the contest. The man asked his name and gave him a new name, Israel, because he had striven with God and men and had prevailed. Jacob named the place Peniel, "for I have seen God face to face, and yet my life is preserved." Yet, the man with whom he had struggled had been a stranger to him. He never learned his name. The man he became was not totally different from the man he was before, but not totally the same either. He became a stranger to his former self.

You and I have no way of knowing whether the man with whom Jacob wrestled until the break of day had any resemblance to Esau. We do know from the record that before this wrestling at Jabbok, Esau had preoccupied Jacob's restless spirit. Approach-avoidance stress and strain beset him as he anticipated meeting his brother. We do know that he was a changed person by reason of his wrestling match with the man whose name he did not know. We do know, also, that when he met his brother Esau, his prayer for deliverance from his brother's hand was answered. ". . . Esau ran to meet him, and embraced him, and fell on his neck and kissed him, and they wept." The ecstatic reconciliation had its beginning in a changed Jacob who met God face to face and lived.

The sweaty crucible of pastoral counseling with a whole family presents powerful family conflicts and rivalries. These, like this classical Old Testament story, make soap operas of both the afternoon and evening varieties on television seem tame, boring, and shallow in comparison. Greed for power and the family fortune underlie many of the facadelike symptoms of sexual acting-out, unremitting self-pity, personality disorders, and even some physical illnesses that families in chaos present to a counselor. The politics of the inner circle of family conflict are *power politics.* Who is going to control whom, and who has to knuckle under to whom? This struggle within the clan and between clans regularly traces back to arguments over the birthright, to occasions of betrayal when trickery took place. Chaos is set in motion by occasions of the purloined blessing.[2]

On rare and unexpected occasions, I have as a pastoral counselor seen tight, irreconcilable situations like these shaken to their foundations by the events of a single, brief period of time. I have seen persons once again find access to and reconciliation with each other. I have sensed that God was present, breaking down barriers that mere rational approaches to human insight could not touch. As I have reflected on the course of the creative renewal of relationships, I have stood amazed at what I saw. As Wordsworth says:

> . . . hearing often times
> The still, sad music of humanity,
> Nor harsh nor grating, though of ample power
> To chasten and subdue. And I have felt
> A presence that disturbs me with the joy
> Of elevated thoughts; a sense sublime
> Of something far more deeply interfused,
> Whose dwelling is the light of setting suns,
> And the round ocean and the living air,
> And the blue sky, and in the mind of man.
> *Lines Composed a Few Miles Above*
> *Tintern Abbey,* 1. 88.

Such a mystical awareness reminds me of the proximate, finite, and limited nature of the purely empirical explanations of personal change in the lives of individuals and families. The life force of the Presence of God in the history of families and individuals reminds the reverent scientist of human relations of the randomness in human life—as opposed to the positivistic predictability of human behavior. As I have quoted Karen Horney before: "Life itself is the great therapist. It is the only one that does not ask those being treated if they will take the treatment." We do not break God's laws, but break ourselves upon them. We are often really thrown out of joint with ourselves and all those whose approval we consider worthwhile. Then, in our wrestling with the messenger of God, we suddenly discover that the bones thrown out of joint are made to praise God. The pastoral counselor himself or herself is not exempt from this strange intervention of the Stranger who meets us and our counselees in the long, dark nights of the human spirit.

CHRIST IN STRANGERS WELCOMED

The occasions of the Presence of God as Stranger thus far discussed have been introduced by evidences from the Old Testament. All of these are more than just slightly related to the instances in the New Testament. The passage in Hebrews is a motif for both the Old and New Testaments: "Do not neglect to show hospitality to strangers, for thereby some have entertained angels unawares." This seems to be an unspoken reference to the strangers whom Abraham and Sarah entertained at the oaks of Mamre. Similarly, in the Last Judgment scene in Matthew 25:35 Jesus says: ". . . I was a stranger and you welcomed me." The Lord Jesus Christ Himself is embodied in the need of the stranger or sojourner at our door. "To welcome," in Greek, is *synagete*, meaning to bring together, call together, in some passages. In this specific case, it means to show kindness and to entertain. These two meanings embrace the whole reverence for the sojourner, the foreigner. The noun form of this verb is *synagoge*, meaning the gathering place for water or a crop, and being the name of the place of worship in which Jesus spoke at Nazareth.

We can remain faithful to the text and assume that welcoming a stranger means taking persons who are foreign to us and our way of life into our community. It means creating for them a fellowship that offsets their loneliness and becomes an antidote for their feelings of not belonging, of being different, unusual, and alien. In his letter to the Ephesians, Paul says that Jesus came and preached peace both to those who were far off and to those who were near. "So then," he says, "you are no longer strangers and sojourners, but you are fellow citizens with the saints and members of the household of God . . ." (2:19).

The present-day concern among many pastoral counselors is for a systems approach to the care and counseling of individuals and families. It is not enough merely to deal with an individual apart from the system of his or her family. Nor can the family be adequately cared for pastorally without exploring their relationships to the church, the school, the state, and federal systems that interlock with the family as it seeks to function and grow. As John Donne said, "No man is an island, entire of itself."

The stranger whom we welcome is out of touch with his or her life-support system. The purpose and function of effective and lasting pastoral counseling is for the pastoral counselor to decrease, while the gathered community of a life-support system to whom he or she has introduced the stranger increases. To see the Living Christ in a stranger is not enough. To welcome him or her into a living support system of the gathered community of faith is imperative.

This dimension of pastoral counseling points to the flaw in the so-called "private practice" of pastoral counseling when it is done apart from vital access to a community of faith. When this happens, to call what is being done *pastoral* counseling is a contradiction of terms, because the community of a shared faith is that into which the stranger, the alien, is welcomed.

Yet, this ushers in a paradoxical effect. When we bring contemporary pastoral counseling practice into dialogue with "welcoming the Christ in strangers," immediately the situation of the person's first conversation with a pastoral counselor comes to mind. Even if you have known them for many years, they feel strange, awkward, and out of place in this new relationship. You are meeting them at the level of their personal, private world of distress. One of their inner communications with themselves is that no one has ever been miserable in the particular way they are. They are strange, unusual, and odd. They may ask: "You have never seen anybody as mixed up as I am, have you?" They may not *want* to be a part of a fellowship of suffering people. In fact, they may feel themselves to be "special" in the uniqueness of their suffering. They may flatter you by saying that they came to you because it would take a person with your experience, expertise, and prestige to care for them. You begin to shift from side to side in your chair because their flattery makes you uncomfortable. Your capacity for hospitality is severely tested.

Then, too, your welcome of them is tried more intensely when their particular story is in deed and fact stranger than anything you have ever before heard or seen. Internally, you are flabbergasted because you had been sailing along somewhat bored by the monotony of the kinds of complaints your counselees have been presenting. You, in your vanity, had begun to assume that you had "seen it all" and that there is nothing new under the sun. Now, you are presented this outlandish thing. You are even repulsed by the whole story. At just this moment, you have met a stranger. It is difficult for you to believe the Living Christ is present in this pseudonymous, strange, foreign being sitting across the room from you. What on earth do you do?

I have been in this dilemma more times than I like to remember. The Presence of Christ here is no "sweet, sweet spirit in this place." When I begin to feel these profound repugnancies, I like to remind myself of what Moses did when he saw a strange phenomenon in the burning bush: "I will turn aside and see this great sight, why the bush is not burnt."

To turn aside from my fixed and well-acquainted ways of doing things, understanding people, and stereotypical thinking (and to marvel at the strange phenomenon my counselee or visitor has presented me) is a discipline of great worth to cultivate. Edmund Husserl, from a much different philosophical framework, calls this "bracketing" and "disciplined naíveté." He says: "We do not abandon the thesis we have adopted, we make no change in our conviction. . . . we set it, as it were, 'out of action,' we 'disconnect it,' 'bracket it.' " Having done this, we take a childlike attitude of open, welcoming empathy for the strange person sitting across from us. We "make room" for them in our world. As we do so, we are promised that we will see the Lord Jesus Christ.[3]

Another facet of the meeting of a pastoral counselor with a stranger is that he or she may need desperately for you or me to be a stranger to them. They may tell you of person after person in their friendship and work associate groups to whom they could have talked "if they had not known them so well." They need a person who does not know them, who for all personal purposes is foreign to their world, a "neutral" ear. A complex set of motivations intertwine themselves in this expression of the counselee. One is the legitimate hunger for someone who will hear "their side" of their situation. They do not feel that they have "had a hearing."

Another motivation is their distrust of people, in general, and those, in particular, whom they know well. Then, again, they want someone with whom they can confer, to whom they can confess, and whom they do not have to face again. People whose present circumstance is so tabooed by society that it cuts them off from their known community need a "place of refuge" to which they can go and entrust themselves in the hands of unbiased strangers.

Such was the need of the apostle Paul after his conversion. The Living Christ urged him to seek out Ananias in Damascus. For centuries, the Catholic confessional met this need in its anonymity. The sometimes harsh and arbitrary "rule" of some psychoanalytically oriented psychiatrists to converse with no one but their patient about his or her problems nevertheless addresses this need of the patient for a stranger who is uninvolved in their sphere of friends and relatives. The obverse side of this "rule" is that the patients or counselees will talk only to the analyst about their problems. Thus, they ostensibly do not "drain off" their energies from the analytic relationship by chattering indiscriminately with anyone and everyone.

Pastoral counseling necessarily provides the positive feature of the psychotherapists without, hopefully, being distorted by "buying into" the system "lock, stock, and barrel." One of the reasons pastoral counseling centers have become widely used and meaningful sources of help to individuals and families is that persons can receive intensive personal attention in an anonymous setting. The need of the counselee not only to be a stranger, but also to have the counselor be a stranger, places a unique burden of responsibility upon us as ministers of reconciliation "in Christ's own stead."

THE IN-GROUP AND THE STRANGER

When we come into the world as newborn infants, the long-range intention of God in both creation and redemption, in both our biological destiny and our spiritual maturity, is that we move from the necessary bonding to our mothers to an increasingly wider world of loving attachments. In the vicissitudes of the parent-child interaction, rejection, ridicule, or physical abuse turns the parent of a child into a stranger.

Andras Angyal aptly observes that the much publicized Oedipal situation of the attachment of a child to one or the other parent is a great deal more than the specific sexual and gender aspects of the relationship. Adding any outsider to the original dyad is, in effect, to take in or welcome a stranger.

Early in his or her growth, a male or female child is called upon in the very biology of the relationship to welcome strangers, in the other parent and in the siblings. The new member—the father, the new sibling—is at first experienced as an intruding stranger. When he or she is able to "achieve integration within the larger family group, the others cease to be strangers and become parts of his (or her) home." [4] This process, I might add, continues throughout a person's life. He or she is called upon repeatedly to break out of the safe confines of the people who are known and to become related to strange people. Gaining access to the larger family of humankind means leaving father, mother, brother, and sister and incorporating one's life with strangers.

To mature sexually, one must go to a stranger. The conventional ethic throughout the Scripture is that sex is both taboo with one's blood kin and with someone who is "strange" and has not first been welcomed into the gathered community of each other's relatives, friends, and neighbors. In terms of the creation of humankind in the image of God, the male and female dimensions of this image are strangers to each other and themselves until they find each other and become known to each other in terms of their responsible life-support communities of faith. Beyond this come the strangeness of bond and free, Jew and Gentile, as well as male and female who cease to be strangers and become known to each other. In these welcomings, we see Jesus Christ, and His Presence blesses us.

A final Gospel account of an event demonstrates the mystery of the elusive Presence of God in pastoral counseling. That is the story of the two persons walking on the road to Emmaus, talking of the things that had happened in the news they had received of the Resurrection of Jesus. A stranger, whom they thought to be a visitor or sojourner, "drew near and went with them." They quickly encompassed him in their confidence, even though "their eyes were kept from recognizing him." They continued with him until they came to their village. There they urged him to stay with them because the day was now far spent. As they sat down to eat together, they recognized him, and he eluded their vision. Their main memory of him was that he opened their eyes to the Scriptures (Luke 24:13–32).

In some sectors of the whole field of pastoral counseling today, the Scriptures are taken as the primary focus of pastoral counselors. However, we can easily slide into making of the Scriptures an inquisitor's law book and making of the pastoral counseling relationship a moral inquisition. The Hobart Mowrer and Jay Adams schools of counseling can be cited as psychological authority for doing this.

The Scriptures, indeed, do provide all that we need to know and far more about behaviorally patterning our lives to a transformed life in Christ. However, our eyes can still be closed to the Living Presence of the Resurrected Christ. When we and our counselees walk together toward our particular village, the Bible is essentially a closed book to us until we are caught up together in the Presence of the Resurrected Christ. Then, we have our eyes opened to the meaning of the Scriptures as a whole, i.e., He lived out the intention of God in such a way that it was necessary that He endure the Cross, die, be buried, and rise again. Therefore, both we and our counselee abide alone, unless we, like a grain of wheat, die daily in our own self-absorbed narcissism and are raised to walk in the newness of life.

The central and living truth of the Scripture does not begin with a book, a theory of inspiration, but with an eye-opening, personal encounter with the Resurrected Lord Jesus Christ. The Resurrection, not as a doctrine but as a living event, creates a light that causes everyone in the Bible to cast a shadow. Jesus, the Christ, is the good and perfect gift who comes "down from the Father of lights with whom there is no variation or shadow due to change" (James 1:17).

The Presence of God
in Listening, Silence,
and Community

*And behold, the Lord passed by, and a great strong wind rent
the mountain, and broke in pieces the rocks before the Lord, but
the Lord was not in the wind; and after the wind an earthquake,
but the Lord was not in the earthquake; and after the earthquake
a fire, but the Lord was not in the fire; and after the fire, the
sound of utmost silence. And when Elijah heard it, he wrapped
his face in his mantle and went out and stood at the entrance to
the cave. And behold, there came a voice to him, and said, "What
are you doing here, Elijah?"*

*1 Kings 19:11–12 (translation by Samuel Terrien, The Elusive
Presence, p. 232)*

A spirit glided past my face;
    the hair of my flesh stood up.
It stood still, but I could not discern
    its appearance.
A form was before my eyes;
    there was silence, then I heard a voice:
"Can mortal man be righteous
    before God?
Can a man be pure before his maker?"
Job 4:15–17

*If he listens to you, you have gained your brother. But if he does
not listen, take one or two others along with you. . . . For where
two or three are gathered in my name, there I am in the midst
of them.*

Matthew 18:15–16, 20

5
The Presence of God in Listening, Silence, and Community

Since the emergence of pastoral counseling as a personal and pastoral discipline into the life of the Christian fellowship, the importance of silence in the relationship of counselor to counselee has been repeatedly emphasized. From the beginning of my ministry as a pastoral counselor, both the spiritual and the empirical dimensions of silence, listening, and spiritual "waiting" have been central to my faith and practice as a pastor.

One of the earliest counselees who entrusted his spiritual concerns to me was a first-year seminarian. He had always leaned dependently and slavishly upon parents, pastors, college professors, and—now—seminary professors to motivate him to do his work. The first three interviews I had with him consisted of his demanding specific instruction in how to meet this responsibility and to please those professors. He haltingly gained a measure of insight into his dependent way of life. On the fourth interview, he came in and sat down. Immediately he said: "I have decided that I have been coming to talk with you just to get on the good side of you, just as I did with my pastor and with my college professors."

I said to him: "Then you have been pretty eager to get my approval?" A long, painful silence ensued. I felt uneasy, impatient, and even hostile during the first part of the silence. Then, I remembered my training, which had taught me that silence could uncover what speech would hide. In the second part of the silence, a change took place in me. I began to feel some genuine compassion for this person. I turned my thoughts upward in prayer as I remained silent. During this silence, the man got up and walked out of the room. I continued in my silent meditation and prayer for awhile before I returned to other duties.

Two weeks later, the student sought another appointment, which I readily gave him. In this interview he told me: "During that very talkative (laughingly) discussion we had the last time we were together, I need to tell you that when I came to see you I had already decided to come into your office, get you to talking, and, then, in the middle of what you were saying, I would get up and walk out. I was going to do that to let you and myself know that I need not be dependent on you. But when I started the conversation, you just sat silently. At first, I felt that your silence was an unfriendly silence. It suddenly changed and became a friendly silence. I still had to do what I had decided to do—leave. In your friendly silence I left, knowing without your saying so that you would understand."

The reality of silence is no mere "gimmick" for manipulating people. For it to be meaningful, a listening silence must transcend the dreary fate of being a "technique" of pastoral counseling. It becomes a spiritual discipline of patience, prayer, and long-suffering in "waiting before God." Yearning for the Presence of God can turn the pastoral counseling relationship from a dialogue into a trialogue. The wisdom of counselee and counselor both are shifted out of a sapiential mode (i.e., personal wisdom), into the mode of a meeting in the Presence of the Eternal God.

Concentrating intently upon the Presence of God in silence, listening, and questing for a community of spiritual kinfolk renews us as pastoral counselors and sets our counselees free of their bondage.

BIBLICAL AND CLINICAL CONVERGENCES

In the previous chapter, I used the metaphor, "coalescence," to symbolize the "growing together" into one body we experience. The understandings we gain from the Scriptures "coalesce" with that which we receive from our clinical work as pastoral counselors. In this chapter, let me use another metaphor, i.e., the convergence of two separate perspectives into one composite vision of biblical and clinical reality. In both of these metaphors, you may readily identify the "method of correlation" of Paul Tillich. The questions which arise from the day-to-dayness of being a pastoral counselor are correlated with the substance of the Christian faith.

THE CONVERGENCE OF PASTORAL ISOLATION WITH A PROPHETIC COMMUNITY

"WHAT ARE YOU DOING HERE?"

When you and I committed ourselves to the disciplines of pastoral counseling, we had to "stand on our own," with a minimum of spiritual and financial support from our faith communities. It was an exercise in independence, an exciting adventure in austere survival. As we counsel with people, counseling is often a "testing of the Baals" of idolatrous relationships such as I described in the previous chapter. Such work is a single-handed effort. The isolation easily turns into loneliness. Therefore, we form pastoral counseling associations that easily become "flat earths" beyond which we cannot see.

We did not really face the necessity for "standing on our own" before God. We shifted our dependency to a hospital counseling center, a seminary faculty, a large system of pastoral counseling centers, the American Association of Pastoral Counselors, a medical center, or something else. When we, for any reason, become alienated from this particular "flat earth," we fall into despair. We cannot see the galaxies of the universe of the Eternal beyond our present set of relationships. You might say, in the terms of 1 Kings 19, that we move from the Mount Carmel of "testing the Baals" to the Mount Hebron of isolation and despair.

One of the most intriguing instances of the Presence of God

in a time of silence is that of Elijah at the entrance to the cave on Mount Horeb, the mount of God. In the depths of his despair from his flight from the avenging hand of Jezebel after his decimation of her priests on Mount Carmel, Elijah said in his prayer: ". . . I, even I only, am left; and they seek my life, to take it away." The prophet was commanded to stand on the mountain before Yahweh, literally, "in the presence of Yahweh." The "Lord passed by" (1 Kings 19:10, 11). As Samuel Terrien says: "After three negative phrases, the positive statement provides the key to the understanding of the whole narrative: 'And after the fire, the sound of utmost silence. . . . It is a silence which may—so to speak—be 'cut with a knife.' " [1]

Yahweh gives Elijah specific guidance to anoint Hazael as king of Damascus, Jehu as king of Israel, and Elisha as his own successor. He infused His purpose in history into Elijah's brilliant but helpless spirit. Then He commanded him to seek out the seven thousand in Israel who, in spite of Jezebel, had not bowed to Baal nor kissed him. As Terrien again says, this "germinated in the following centuries the notion of the 'remnant,' a community of the faithful which could survive the destruction of the state and the annihilation of the cultus. That remnant could potentially explode the restrictiveness of an ethnic community. Here we witness the birth of the idea of *ecclesia,* an assembly of those who trust their God rather than submit to the tyranny of political or institutional conformism." [2] To use Jesus' metaphor, it was a new wineskin for the new wine of a new covenant.

This unique story speaks to the transforming possibilities of the revelation of the Living God to the committed pastoral counselor when he or she becomes depressed, discouraged, beleaguered, and helpless. This happens after grueling contests with the spirit of heaviness that hangs persistently upon one counselee after another. The isolation of the pastoral counselor himself or herself contributes to this despair. The heavy demands of counselees and the lack of support from organized churches, associations of churches, and denominational sources of support converge upon one another to undercut the morale of a pastoral counselor. In some cases, he or she is too dependent upon the money and inspiration of his or her counselees to keep going financially and spiritually.

Similarly, the pastoral counselor of today is, by the nature

of his or her calling, "paddling upstream" against the tide of
popular, civil religion. A considerable number of those to whom
we minister are persons who have suffered much at the hands
of such pseudoreligion. They often have appealed to the church
for understanding and been given a stone rather than bread. The
god they have learned about bears only a slight resemblance to
the God and Father of our Lord Jesus Christ as portrayed in
the New Testament. In fact, the more brutal passages in the
Old Testament are benign in comparison to the demands of the
gods that appear in the anguish of our counselees' desperation
for acceptance, forgiveness, personal worthiness, and self-esteem.
We are called upon singlehandedly to wrestle with, conquer, and
break the spell of the Baals whom they worship. They themselves
are so trapped in their bondage to that which they have had
pounded into their ears that they rarely can join in a therapeutic
alliance with us. They expect us to do this *for* them more often
than not.

What if you, as a pastoral counselor, should have the privilege
of mounting a political offensive against such teaching in homes
and from the pulpits? You soon would find enough opposition
that you, like Elijah, would need to run for forty days and nights
in search of safety. Then, you would cry out to God, as he did:
"I, even I only, am left."

Pushed to this extreme, you "hit bottom." Then, in silence,
God comes to you in a way you have not known before. You
discover, as Elijah did, that you are not alone. If you have the
foresight of Elijah to seek the face of God in a wilderness of
your own choosing, you are likely to be called by name: "What
are you doing here?" As you search yourself for a clear answer
to this question, you will be recommissioned to go back and
find that "remnant" of persons who have not bowed the knee
to Baal.

In times of intense conflict, I have had to stand alone to deal
with the ecclesiastical pressures that threatened my whole ministry of pastoral care and counseling. I have found that a *retreat*
to a wilderness was imperative. I saturated myself in solitude.
As I have nurtured silence in my noisy heart, I have encountered
the instructions of the Living God. Clearly, the Spirit of God
has caused me to think: "What are you doing here?" Then I
have been led back to the arena of conflict.

There I found an *ecclesia* of strong and reliable persons. They have labored together with me to bring a whole new Gestalt of grace into the system of relationships they provided. The old conflicts subsided into insignificance. The God of grace and glory poured upon His people His power. He brought the church's bud to glorious flower as He granted us wisdom and courage to face that hour.

I learned that meeting God in silence, when all the contending voices, including mine, have been hushed, was the imperative. Then the church, the *ecclesia,* is an event. The church is where God chooses it to happen, and not necessarily where people say that it is.

Likewise, I have had the privilege of conferring with other pastoral counselors in such times of distress. One man, in particular, grants me permission to tell you of his struggle. He had been a pastor of several churches. He took his training in formal pastoral counseling at a particular training center. Upon completion of his training, he moved to a nearby city and started a pastoral counseling service, gaining exceptional community support. He did this under the auspices of the training center in which he had been trained.

The more he succeeded, the more opposition he received from within this training center's power structure. As this tension mounted, his home began to disintegrate. He was in despair both in his work and in his home, becoming more isolated by the day. He went into therapy himself, from which he received much insight and personal support.

The conflict at work and in his home intensified, however. He resigned from his job as director of the center and divorced his wife. He was alone. This was his wilderness of Horeb. He began to search for spiritual renewal. He says that Elijah's words from the Lord fitted him: "What are you doing here?"

Then, friends whom he had known for ten to fifteen years reached out to him. They offered him a whole new context for his ministry, with a patterned plan for his continued growth and advancement. In this reborn world, he discovered a new community of grace and creativity that affirmed his past spiritual heritage and pointed him to creative development of latent, unused gifts he did not know he had. He likens this era of his life to "another conversion" in which the Presence of God was profoundly felt.

THE PASTORAL COUNSELOR'S OWN THERAPY/SUPERVISION

"NOW IT HAS COME TO YOU"

The more a pastoral counselor serves other people, the more he or she sees himself or herself in the mirrors of the counselees' stories. Their resistances call out our resistances. Ordinarily, the knee-jerk response of fellow pastoral counselors is that when the kinds of troubles our counselees present "now come to us," we ourselves need supervision and personal therapy.

We "Jobs" are programmed to seek supervision and/or therapy from our versions of Eliphaz, Bildad, and Zophar. The *lifelong, endless* expectation that therapy and/or supervision will meet every need, with no emphasis on the relationship of a person to God at all, is a vain hope. Therapy and/or supervision has a beginning, middle, and end. Adoption of therapy/supervision as a permanent way of life is what I am challenging.

The sound of silence in the Presence of God is also found in Eliphaz the Temanite's words as he speaks to Job as a friend in Job 4:1–21. He is careful of Job's privacy in his pain. He asks if he can venture a word with him without offending him. He tells Job that Job has instructed many, strengthened their weak hands, upheld the stumbling, and made firm feeble knees. Now, the same things have come to him, and he is impatient. After a few words of conventional wisdom, Eliphaz shifts away from trite phrases to tell about his own personal meeting with God. A spirit glided past his face. It scared him so much that his hair stood on end. "There was a silence, then I heard a voice: 'Can mortal man be righteous before God? Can a man be pure before his maker?' "

Out of the silence came the message of the Lord reminding him of what someone has called "the eternal qualitative difference between the Creator and the creature." God is righteous and we are unrighteous; God is pure and we are impure; God is boundless and we are limited; God faints not and neither is He weary—and we get tired and need rest. Yet, this remains a secret to us until we hit our limits. Job had come to his limits, presumably as had Eliphaz the Temanite. Regardless of God's transcendence, yet this Creator, says Norman Habel, "is not a high god who has left the earth to run on predetermined principles of wisdom, but one who is involved in all social, personal, and natural processes." [3] The Presence of God met Eliphaz in silence.

Eliphaz could, as well, have been talking to you and me as contemporary pastoral counselors. Our own personal lives are from one season to another often in total disarray from one disaster after another. We have instructed, strengthened, upheld, and steadied others. Now "it has come to us." The shoe is on the other foot! We have been tempted to curse God and die. Yet, we would lash back at our friends who stand in for Eliphaz and say, as Job did: ". . . Worthless physicians are you all. Oh that you would keep silent, and it would be your wisdom!" (Job 13:4–5). Then again, can we take our own medicine and keep silent? Can we concentrate on listening rather than speaking? The Presence of God most often is in the silence, not the words.

In contemporary pastoral counseling, we have devised a trite truism all our own. We assume that when we ourselves are in dire straits, the panacea is to undergo endless therapy ourselves. I am confident that every professional who cares for other people needs mentors with whom he or she can regularly consult. These mentors are sustaining graces to us in time of need. We are tremendously vulnerable to our own loss of perspective when we "go it alone" as pastoral counselors. Yet, to replace your own judgment with that of a "therapist" and/or to be in "supervision" forever leads to a loss of confidence in our own decisions, sloppiness in the discipline of researching our own work, and to a work paralysis. Speaking or acting of ourselves, apart from a supervisor, becomes difficult.

The more insidious deficit, however, is that we avoid our own wilderness. We do not seek the face of God in silence. The specific antidote for overdependence upon therapists and supervisors is an individual *retreat* to a wilderness of our own choosing. Gethsemane Monastery in Bardstown, Kentucky, Laity Lodge in Kerrville, Texas, or one of the many Yokefellow Institutes provide such an atmosphere. You may choose your own personal place of solitude, such as a wilderness park, a chosen "Bethel" or "Horeb" from your past experiences with God. A sabbatical at

St. John's College in Collegeville, Minnesota, provides a longer time of spiritual self-encounter with God. A living record of such a retreat is Henri Nouwen's *Genesee Diary*.

The prophetic heart of pastoral counseling beats in rhythm when, in the depths of silence before the Presence of God, we "face up," as Eliphaz did, to our impermanence and tawdry omnipotence, our frail mortality, and the impurity of our motives. Our perspective is restored; our sense of humor and capacity to laugh at ourselves is rekindled. Confidence in this wisdom is enriched. We are led to an *ecclesia* of other seekers after the face of God and become colleagues with them. As for supervision, such an end-state is the goal of genuine, unpretentious supervision.

Recently, the rediscovery of the importance of spirituality in the life and work of the pastoral counselor has begun to take place. National and regional meetings have been increasingly committed to this quest. The work of Henri Nouwen has been a welcomed infusion of spiritual grace into our life together. The re-centering of pastoral counseling in the disciplines of the very Presence of God through serious study of the prophets, of Jesus, and of the apostles will give substance and direction to this quest.

LISTENING AND THE PRESENCE OF GOD

Reconciliation of people who are finding fault with each other makes up a large part of the pastoral counseling load. Rarely do these persons deal with each other face to face. When they do, they do not deal with each other gently, looking to themselves and the particular ways in which they are being tempted. They have trouble listening closely to what the other person has to say and speaking in such a way as to be heard. Yet, each person in the conflict deeply wishes to "be heard out," feels misunderstood and unappreciated, wounded and weary.

This is another common clinical situation hurting for the entry of the Presence of God in Jesus Christ as it is set forth in the Gospels. In the Matthew 18 account, a persistent refrain about *listening* appears. Jesus as a twelve-year-old person is portrayed by Luke as being found by His parents in the temple, "sitting among the teachers, listening to them and asking them questions." This is a clue to His "silent years," that is, the years of which we have no record but the one in Luke 2:41–51 as to what His years of personality development were like. We do know that He listened and asked questions.

His understanding and answers were astounding. Mark (9:2–8), Luke (9:28–36), and Matthew (16:24–28) tell us of the Transfiguration of Jesus in that astounding epiphany in which a voice came from the clouds saying: "This is my beloved Son, with whom I am well pleased; listen to him." Raphael paints this scene in unison with the story of the disciples' frustrated attempt to heal the epileptic boy when He told His disciples that this kind of healing comes only by prayer and fasting.

Mary, the sister of Martha, sat at Jesus' feet and listened to Him. Many of His disciples said of His teaching: "This is a hard saying, who can listen to it?" Jesus did not lament in sorrow when they had trouble listening to Him, but told them that even more difficult things were in the making for them.

In turn, those who benefited by His ministry of healing, such as the man who was blind from birth, had difficulty in getting others to listen to what they told them. They asked Him: "What did he do to you?" He answered: "I have told you already, and you would not listen. Why do you want to hear it again? Do you too want to become his disciples?" (John 9:26–27).

Even more difficult than this, the followers of Jesus in the gathered community of faith had real trouble listening to each other. Apparently, this occurred when they had offended each other. Jesus' prescription for the healing of their sense of community with each other was centered upon getting each other to listen. "If your brother sins against you, go and tell him his fault, between you and him alone. If he listens to you, you have gained your brother. But if he does not listen, take one or two others along with you, that every word may be confirmed by the evidence of two or three witnesses. If he refuses to listen to them, tell it to the church; and if he refuses to listen even to the church, let him be to you as a Gentile and a tax collector" (Matthew 18:15–17). In each instance, the objective of the conversation is to enable the other to listen. The pattern Jesus prescribes is the narrow gate through which Christians enter into fellowship with each other.

Douglas Steere describes the intricate difficulty of such listening: "A Finn once suggested to me that in every conversation between two people there are always at least six persons present. What each person said are two; what each person meant to say are two more; and what each person understood the other to say are two more. There is certainly no reason to stop at six, but the fathomless depth of the listener who can go beyond words, who can even go beyond the conscious meanings behind words and who can listen with the third ear for what is unconsciously being meant by the speaker, this fashion of attentive listening furnishes a climate where the most unexpected disclosures occur that are in the way of being miracles in one sense, and the most natural and obvious things in the world, on the other." [4]

He goes even further into the complexity of listening and being heard when he says that each of us has an "inner spectator listener" who listens to what he himself or herself is saying as it is said. I would observe that this is not an evenly distributed capacity from person to person. I often wonder if many people really pay that much attention to what they themselves are saying. I have heard people say many things, apparently unaware of what they were saying. They said exactly what they thought *before* they thought it!

The apostle Peter spoke at the Transfiguration, saying: "Master, it is well that we are here; let us make three booths, one for you, one for Moses, and one for Elijah." Mark adds: "For he did not know what to say, for they were exceedingly afraid." Matthew and Luke omit this comment from their account, although all three writers agree that the disciples were frightened.

It does seem to me that either the absence or the denial of the "inner spectator listener," as Steere describes it, lets hurtful and even deceitful things be said in a callous and unfeeling way often unremembered by the person who said them. He or she never heard themselves say it! When confronted, they will deny it in all honesty!

Jesus says that the objective is to get the person to listen, either on a one-to-one, a threesome, or a communal basis. This pattern is a working design of what happens in the pastoral task of conflict resolution. The contentions that arise between warring factions in the local church congregation, the disagreements, quarrels, and running battles between family members consume much of a pastor's time and energy. The formal work of pastoral counseling is individual counseling, conjoint counseling of twosomes or dyads, usually husband and wife, or group and/or family counseling. Getting these persons to *listen* to themselves and to each other is what pastoral counseling is all about.

Much training in pastoral counseling and psychotherapy is overdependent upon Greek patterns of life interpretation in which "knowing" and "seeing" are the primary concerns in effecting change in human lives. In a rebound against this emphasis, other forms of training emphasize positive vs. negative reinforcement of adaptive and maladaptive behaviors, with little attention to insight. Contrary to both these angles of vision, the biblical goal is to get the person to listen, to be reconciled, to forgive, and to establish a new covenant of trust with real people in his or her world.

Forming a covenant of trust "binds" people to each other in forgiveness, with a long-range intention of doing so "seventy times seven." Forgiving an offending person has to be done by your "inner spectator listener" again and again within the privacy of your own prayers.

The Presence of Christ and Listening

Once again, the ministry of reconciliation and redirection of life is centered in the realization of the Presence of the Living Christ. After having prescribed the one-to-one, threesome, and communal quest for listening, Jesus says that "where two or three are gathered in my name, there I am in the midst of them." This much quoted promise is rarely seen or discussed in the context of the disciplines of listening to each other. These disciplines are preludes to our meeting the Presence of Christ in the gathered community of listeners.

In family counseling as done by a pastoral counselor, it seems to me that a more transpersonal approach to family conflict would be to take the paradigm that Jesus prescribes as the "upfront," explicit agenda at the beginning of the process. You and I would state our aim to produce face-to-face conversation among the family, to encourage them not only to say their minds to each other, but to listen to each other and enable each other to listen. The ultimate goal would be to seek the Presence of God, who in Jesus Christ has promised to be in our midst.

Another kind of consultation being done, more often by highly disciplined pastoral counselors, is conflict resolution among church members who are at odds with each other. Here, to be explicit about the paradigm of Jesus, is a form of ethical confrontation difficult to surpass. Coupling this with our own role-modeling of the companion teachings of the apostle Paul in Galatians 6:1–10 is a powerful stimulus to realistic reconciliation.

I have been in many churches where moderate to severe hostility between factions of members reigned over all functions of the church. I have also seen the same phenomenon in colleges, seminaries, medical schools, and mental health organizations. At the acute stages of these conflicts, I have had the fantasy of everyone imposing upon himself or herself a rule of silence for at least a week. Then the Eternal might appear to all of us.

This fantasy of mine reminded me of the powerful story of the opening of the seven seals in the Revelation of John. The story builds in tension and awesomeness to the opening of the last, the seventh seal. Then it says: "When the Lamb opened the seventh seal, there was silence in heaven for about half an hour" (Revelation 8:1). When the people of God are at war with themselves, it seems to me that even a half-hour of silence would give them a chance to experience the Presence of God. As Job says, our silence could be our teacher.

Yet, as I push my seemingly impossible fantasy further, I am aware that such a silence before God can issue into a severe mercy from God. The grimmer aspect of considering a person who resolutely refuses to listen to anyone as "a Gentile and a tax collector" is grief-strickening to a sensitive congregation. It introduces the ambiguous responsibility of church discipline of an individual or group of individuals. We learn much about this from the Spirit-centered fellowships, such as the Society of Friends, the Mennonites, and the Hutterites.

Silence, listening, and the sense of community are brought into being by the Presence of God. Thus, God moves in the life of a pastoral counselor in the crucial human situations of pastoral counseling.

The "Over-Againstness" and the "Alongsideness" of the Presence of God

*At a lodging place on the way the Lord met him and sought to
kill him.*

Exodus 4:24

*And the Lord said to Moses, "This very thing that you have spoken
I will do; for you have found favor in my sight, and I know you
by name." Moses said, "I pray thee, show me thy glory." And
he said, "I will make all my goodness pass before you, and will
proclaim before you my name 'The Lord'; and I will be gracious
to whom I will be gracious, and will show mercy on whom I will
show mercy. But," he said, "you cannot see my face; for man
shall not see me and live."*

Exodus 33:17–20

*Such was the appearance of the likeness of the glory of the Lord.
And when I saw it, I fell upon my face, and I heard the voice
of one speaking. And he said to me, "Son of man, stand upon
your feet, and I will speak with you." And when he spoke to
me, the Spirit entered into me and set me upon my feet; and I
heard him speaking to me.*

Ezekiel 1:28–2:2

*Jesus answered him, "If a man loves me, he will keep my word,
and my Father will love him, and we will come to him and make
our home with him."*

John 14:23

6
The "Over-Againstness" and the "Alongsideness" of the Presence of God

Two important metaphors of the Presence of God appear in the language of the Old and New Testaments. They are relational metaphors. The first are the Hebrew and Greek words for "face"—*panim* in Hebrew and *prosopon* in Greek. These words are often translated "presence," and, occasionally, "face." Yahweh told Moses: "You cannot see my face, for man cannot see me and live" (Exodus 33:20). Paul says: "God . . . has shone in our hearts to give the light of the knowledge of the glory of God in the face of Jesus Christ."

This metaphor emphasizes the overwhelming *difference* between us and God. We cannot survive in the contrast. Our "over-againstness" as we stand in the Presence of God rocks the things in our lives which can be shaken in order that the things which cannot be moved may remain. The positive, conjunctive emotions associated with such an encounter with God are reverence, awe, and a desire to please God above all others. When we are alienated from God, these feelings turn into terror, a fear of punishment, a suspicion of God, and the paranoid ideation of persecution with a hidden agenda of grandiosity.

The second metaphor is found in the Johannine description of the Holy Spirit as the *parakletos,* the Paraclete, the helper, the one who is "alongside" us, helping us, and being an advocate for us. In the King James Version, this is translated "Comforter." In the Revised Standard Version, it is translated "Counselor." This is not a "face down" over-againstness of God's Presence confronting us. It is a "laboring together" with God as is indicated in 2 Corinthians 5:16–6:10. The conjunctive emotions associated with this relationship to God are intimacy, trust, communion, fellowship, and collaborative effort. When we are alienated from God, these turn into disjunctive emotions of separation, anxiety, loneliness, grief, and even depression.

A process parallel to this "over-againstness" and "alongside-ness" regularly appears between counselors and counselees. The practice of pastoral counseling itself is a "presumptuous" metaphor of the relationship that both the counselee and we ourselves have to God. I say presumptuous in that we *borrow* the authenticity of our stance in relationship to our counselees from both their and our prior existences as selves, either face-to-face with or "alongside" the Living God. It is a holy presumption to say that "God is making His appeal through us as ambassadors for Christ." This is our ultimate certification and our inescapable responsibility at the same time.

Here is my estimate of *the* pastoral ethic of all ethics. Optimumly, we move with the counselees through their and our intrapsychic ghettos, through their and our complaints about spouse, father, mother, and siblings, and into the unlimited vistas of their and our experience with God. Less ideally, counselees expect us magically to change all that displeases them, with no participation on their part. If we refer them and ourselves simultaneously to God, then they expect magical intervention from God. They assert their "entitlement" to be "special" and exempt from any acts of exerted faith.

Two Kinds of Pastoral Counseling Situations

As I review meditatively my whole pastoral counseling load at this time, I find it helpful to assess each situation in the light of the biblical metaphors of the *panim-prosopon* "over-against-ness" of the Presence of God and the *parakletos* "alongsideness" with God. At least two kinds of self-encounter characterize the relationship I have with these persons. In a parallel way, their perceptions and expectations of God correspond.

THE "HELPLESS" AND/OR HOSTILE COUNSELEE

The first kind of counselee place themselves "over-against" us. They may be helpless or compliant to the point of being obeisant and deferential to us. Flattery abounds. They are dependent and passive. They expect us to "fix" them. They persistently expect a "magic word," an ultimate prescription. Underneath all this exterior is a low self-esteem, a personal powerlessness in a threatening world. We may see obvious things that most people can actually do about their situation. We suggest that this is something they can do. They listen with rapt attention. Yet, they never "get around to" doing anything about it.

Such people are clutched by the fear of failure, by the terror of doing something wrong. The pale cast of thought deters them from the path of action, to paraphrase Shakespeare. They are filled with good intentions, but the road to their private torment is paved with these good intentions. They are "over-against" us, themselves, and God. Their internal communication is: "What you say is easy enough for you to say, but it is not in me to do it."

Another kind of counselee is "over-against" us. Such people are extremely self-sufficient, arrogant, and overtly or covertly hostile. They may have come to us because they were given an ultimatum by their parents, their dean, their employer, the law courts, or an insurance company deciding about disability claims. They need us only to please the people who sent them and/or to extract what they want from us. Essentially they are "over-against" us. They do not feel the need nor intention to change in any way. If they have symptoms of depression, it is because they are "in a jam." Since they are not filled with remorse, they feel little need for re-thinking their way of life or learning from their own experience.

Forming a comradeship of spiritual growth (a therapeutic alliance) with these persons is extremely difficult. Our ministry to them is primarily one of crisis intervention, because their lives move from one crisis of their own making to another.

THE COLLABORATIVE COUNSELEE

The second kind of counseling situation presents to us people who are neither helpless nor self-sufficient. Stressed on every side, they are perplexed but not unto despair. They *are* isolated, and the people in their world are "all-demanding" but rarely appreciative, supportive, or empathic. These people come to us much as a player on the field comes out of the game at a "time out" to confer with a coach. They form with us a collaborative relationship; they are "pilgrims on their way." The counselees come to us, to change the figure of speech, as Mr. or Ms. Interpreter. They stop with us for spiritual direction and comparison of maps of the terrain. Assuming that we know the territory, they believe we can listen intently to their confusions, and are not hesitant to provide information, encouragement, and spiritual refreshing on their toilsome way. Yet, they also assume that it is they and not we who are making the journey and carrying the load.

You may readily say: "Such persons as this are healthy. They are not sick. They don't need pastoral counseling." I would respond: "You are right. They *are* productive persons who cannot be classified as 'sick.' They do not need a 'therapist.' They need a *pastor,* though. They need spiritual direction and nutriment. Do they have to come down with 'symptoms' to fit into your or my definition of our task as 'health delivering agents'?"

If so, our idolatry of health has excluded them from our sense of responsibility. These are the "hod carriers" who carry brick in the edification of the people of God. They are the stressed, the strained, the burnt out, the unappreciated, and the unattended. Who are they? They are the professional staff members, the board members, the committee chairpersons, the deacons, the vestry persons, and the lay leaders. They carry the burden in the heat of the day. Who sustains them?

THE PARADOXICAL EXPERIENCE OF GOD'S PRESENCE

I hope that you can resonate with the metaphor of pastoral counseling thus far. To liken pastoral counseling to the paradoxical experience of the "over-againstness" and "alongsideness" of the Presence of God is indeed presumptuous. It is presumptuous in that pastoral counseling is a very fallible, concrete, and "earthy" experience. Yet, the knowledge of God is too high for us. We are dealing with an essentially ineffable or unutterable reality when we dare *speak* of the Presence of God. There is a sense in which *whatever* you or I *say* about God's Presence is not so. "No voice can sing, no heart can frame, nor can the memory find" language that will say the truth, the whole truth, and nothing but the truth about the Presence of God. In fact, this whole book is only a *pointing* toward the Presence of God, destined to be inadequate by the nature of the subject I have chosen.

Consequently, the Bible itself speaks in metaphor of "face-to-faceness" and "side-by-sideness," "over-againstness" and "a-longsideness" about God. The biblical metaphors presume, but they do not pretend to be adequate. Let us explore some of the instances of each side of this paradox found in the Bible. I think we as pastoral counselors will find comradeship with prophetic mentors in the Scriptures.

The dramatic stories of the Old and New Testaments breathtakingly depict the "over-againstness" and the "alongsideness" of the Presence of God and how the one is transformed into the other. In the first place, I want to take a biblical instance of a person "standing over against God" in helplessness and fear and set this in comparison and contrast with a clinical case situation.

Moses was a privileged foster son in the ruling family of Egypt. He saw his Hebrew kinspeople being brutally enslaved by the Egyptians. In a moment of rage, upon seeing one of them being beaten, he "looked this way and that, and seeing no one he killed the Egyptian and hid him in the sand" (Exodus 2:12). "When Pharaoh heard of it, he sought to kill Moses. But Moses fled from Pharaoh, and stayed in the land of Midian" (Exodus 2:15). He married, became a father, and helped his father-in-law, Jethro, the Midianite priest, to tend to his flock.

Finally, God intervened in behalf of the enslaved Israelites in Egypt and appeared to Moses in the epiphany of the burning bush. Moses hid his face, for he was afraid to look at God. In the unrelenting expectation of God that Moses go to deliver His people, Moses became helpless, inadequate, and severely afraid.

He did not know what to say to the Pharaoh. If he knew what to say, he was not eloquent but was slow of speech and tongue.

Yahweh stood "over-against" Moses with awesome demands. Moses was overwhelmed. He reassured Moses, but Moses said: "Oh, my Lord, send, I pray, some other person." The anger of the Lord kindled against Moses. Although He gave Moses Aaron to be a spokesman for him, the account in Exodus 4:24 portrays the Lord as trying to kill Moses! This was a life-and-death encounter of massive proportions.

As time went on in the "over-againstness" of Moses' relationship to Yahweh, the flow of anger ceased to be one-directional. In Numbers 11, Moses heard the people weeping throughout their families, begging for meat to go with the manna. On this occasion, both the Lord *and* Moses were angry: ". . . and the anger of the Lord blazed hotly, and Moses was displeased" (Numbers 11:10). Remarkably, Moses seems to have been displeased, not only with the people but also with the Lord. He complained that too much responsibility had been laid upon his shoulders and that, unless things changed, he *wanted* the Lord to kill him! "I am not able to carry all this people alone, the burden is too heavy for me. If thou wilt deal thus with me, kill me at once, if I find favor in thy sight, that I may not see my wretchedness" (Numbers 11:14–15).

The response of the Lord was not one of "over-againstness," but one of "alongsideness." He gave Moses fellow burden-bearers, even as He later gave to Elijah prophets who had not bowed the knee to Baal. "And the Lord said to Moses, 'Gather for me seventy men of the elders of Israel, whom you know to be the elders of the people and officers over them; and bring them to the tent of meeting, and let them take their stand there with you. And I will come down and talk with you there; and I will take some of the spirit which is upon you and put it upon them; and they shall bear the burden of the people with you, that you may not bear it yourself alone. And say to the people, 'Consecrate yourselves for tomorrow, and you shall eat meat; for you have wept in the hearing of the Lord, saying, 'Who will give us meat to eat? For it was well with us in Egypt.' Therefore the Lord will give you meat, and you shall eat" (Numbers 11:16–18).

Here was a collaborativeness and an "alongsideness" that was born out of the heat of the struggle of the soul of Moses with the Living God. Again and again, the prayer of Moses was: "Now therefore, I pray thee, if I have found favor in thy sight, show me now thy ways, that I may know thee and find favor in thy sight. Consider too that this nation is thy people." And God's promise was: "My presence will go with you, and I will give you rest" (Exodus 33:13–14). Such a metamorphosis of relationship is reminiscent of Whitehead's comment that the process of a person's relationship to God moves from God the enemy, to God the void, to God the friend. A parallel process goes on in the pastoral counseling relationship. If pastoral counselors center the process upon the objective Presence of God in the dialogue, rather than take the burden entirely upon themselves, then other relationships of the counselee become clearer, more easily negotiated, and his or her perspective undergoes more lasting changes.

A CONTEMPORARY "MOSES"

A thirty-two-year-old man was referred to me by the chief of psychiatry in the School of Medicine where I work. The man had been hospitalized amid a psychotic episode. He was married, and he and his wife had two children, ages one and five, a girl and a boy. This patient was delusional and considered to be dangerous to himself and other persons. At first, he seemed to be schizophrenic. As we became better acquainted with him, we discovered he was clearly depressed in a psychotic way.

This man was referred to me because he'd had a rigid religious upbringing and because he had a pronounced sense of mission to liberate the poor and the oppressed. A college graduate and an avid reader of Karl Marx, he was an impassioned opponent of the religious and political establishment. He was also very articulate. Interviews were often devoted to hearing his orations about the injustices being heaped upon the poor.

He gave his own account of his upbringing: "At five months I was in a home essentially broken prior to my birth. My mother, God keep her, was a broken and depressed woman. (At that time she was hospitalized in a state hospital where she stayed for seventeen years before her death.) With my birth there was added responsibility. The 'handwriting was on the wall,' if you will. I was placed in an orphanage in December, 1947, until June, 1949. I did not learn to walk or talk until I was three years old. (Then an uncle and aunt took him into their home.) Home life, work, and discipline went from hard to extreme; usually as money and necessities got lower, the level of violence increased. I was tied in chairs to keep me 'in line.' Handsaws, hammer handles, and electrical light cords were used for whipping and putting the 'fear of God in your hard head.'

"They were right. I *was* fearful of God! I hated Him too! . . . In church I sensed that the Christ of the Gospels was about fairness, but I saw an unjust economic and social order, all too often underwritten by church officials in their public display toward all the children of God. I refused to believe it was 'God's will' that placed me in poverty and as soon as I 'got big' I was going to find who was responsible for this.

"I began early to manifest impulsive, rebellious, and nonconforming mannerisms such as setting fires and putting them out before they got out of control. . . . I was distrustful and hate-filled and found a short reprieve in the social acceptance associated with athletics. Sex was something I did to prove my manhood." (As he reached adulthood, he began to act out his despair with sexual mannerisms that frightened but did no violence to women he met in public.)

Of this habit, he says: "The intensity of that first extremely antisocial act was to go from the clear command to commit that act to a level of volume that came out as static, unintelligible distortions of such magnitude and frequency that spirit would become a dreamlike existence in a battered shell that was supposed to pass for life. That thirteen years of barren, desolate existence (was) held onto with only hope as my constant companion."

He saw entering either the ministry or the military as his only two ways out of what he calls "the harsh realities of 'tobacco road.'" He went into the Marines and was promptly sent to Vietnam. He returned unscathed as far as wounds were concerned, but enraged at the plight of the poverty of the people of Vietnam and the hordes of war orphans, he says.

His efforts in athletics were a temporary solace. His final choice of the military gave some structure to his life. He says that his dedication as an athlete and later his involvement as a Marine precluded any serious or long-term involvement with girls. "Only shallow relationships were tolerated." Yet, in his process of institutionalization in an orphanage as a child and as a patient later, he formed long-term, nonsexual relationships, first to a social worker and then to a woman psychotherapist. His main knowledge about his childhood comes from the social worker with whom he lost touch when he left the orphanage and later met at a boys' home where they were both employed. He stayed in touch with her occasionally until her death.

On the fifth interview, after having told much of the story I have just reported, this man was enough at home with me to blast me out with the anger of his oratory. He had recounted how Karl Marx had taken the part of the poor and oppressed. Professional people like me were comfortable, well-dressed, and living in fine houses with several cars. According to him, I knew nothing about the plight of the poor because I had never known what it was to be hungry, naked, and cold. As he said this he pounded the edge of the desk.

My own heritage rose up to protest. I said: "You are now talking about something of which you are completely ignorant. You have not asked me. You are telling me what *my* heritage is. You are dead wrong. I resent you assuming that because you suffered poverty that you are the only one who has done so. You are shooting your mouth off with ignorance." He was taken aback. He had not known that I, too, could get angry, he said. Then he asked me: "Did you indeed grow up in poverty?" I told him that I did. My purpose here was to care for him and not to unload my life story on him, but it was just too much when he spoke so wrongly of me. (Seven years later, he read my own autobiography, *The Struggle to Be Free,* and called me to compare his story with mine.)

From this point forward, he was not "over-against" me in his sessions with me. He came "alongside" me as a fellow struggler. He very intentionally began to contrast Karl Marx and Jesus, whereas, before this he had seen them as the same—both of them giving their lives to the poor. He could not appreciate Jesus' nonviolence. Injustice had to be overcome by force. This he contended, even though he was, by this time, attending worship services with us at my church by his own choice (I had invited him to do so).

Several months passed while he busied himself on a new job,

on which he was elected a labor steward. He lost interest in the church and became intensely involved in the Socialist Workers' Party in our town.

Then his marriage became unstable. His care of his children was more and more a bone of contention with his wife. They sought family counseling in a child evaluation center. In the crisis, he decompensated and became emotionally disorganized again. He called me for a conference, at which time he told me of a plan to kill a wealthy person in our city who was running for political office. He felt that violence was necessary to set things right for the poor. I firmly disagreed with him and persuaded him to let me help him be admitted to the hospital. He did so, and I stayed in touch with him by telephone. He recompensated and returned to his job without penalty.

He confided in me later that he was testing my acceptance of him and wanted to know for sure that I would stay by him at his worst. He said that I had stood the test. He explained it this way: "You came down off your professional 'high-horse' and cast your lot with me."

He has finally concluded that the ultimate difference between Jesus' and Karl Marx's concern for the poor shows that Jesus took up His cross and suffered with and for the poor. He did *not* resort to violence. Now, this man's concern focuses on the peace movement, and he considers war as the major source of human suffering and privation. He actively engages in peace organizations in our city. He will always be a "son of contention," as was Jeremiah, but he walks in fellowship "alongside" Jesus as the Christ and not "over-against" Him. He has not had a psychotic break in four years.

Upon presenting him with this manuscript for his correction, approval, and permission to publish his story, he had several observations: "The times of severe illness were times when my rage was on a destructive course. But at the core of my illness were some very valid convictions." He reminded me about telling of one occasion when he decided to go on a hunger fast to protest the neglect of the poor in our city. He reminded me that I had said: "Be sure to keep your fluids up to offset dehydration, and I will miss meals regularly, too!" This, I recalled, I had done. I recognized the validity of his "at-the-core" convictions and did not disparage them, but affirmed them. He continued: "But

I lacked the courage and the discipline to find a constructive way to express my need to 'go public' and to do something constructive with my rage.

"Now I find great comfort in being a part of a Quaker meeting. They insist on a person being quite personal in his or her faith in God. I have given up the embarrassing sexual habits and have started using my pen instead as a way of expressing my feelings to people."

He handed me a 95-page, carefully prepared manuscript in which he had written a few pages a week after his work hours.

He is a contemporary Moses who is on his way, through writing, to finding people who will follow him. However, he has found fellowship with other seekers, such as myself, as is evident in his participation in the Quaker meeting. I see him as having demanded a pastoral counselor who would walk "alongside" him and not "over-against" him. This I shall continue to try to be to him.

SHIFTING

The experience of Moses and the counselee just described *shifted* from being "over-against" God's Presence to one of being "alongside" Him in their common task of liberation of the oppressed people. They had in common their conquest of rage as well. The *shift* is indigenous to the experience of the Presence of God and to the parallel process in pastoral counseling.

Ezekiel made this shift more instantaneously. The Presence of God came to him "like the appearance of the bow that is in the cloud on the day of rain, so was the appearance of the brightness round about" (Ezekiel 1:28). Then he tells of his dramatic "shift" from helplessness to collaboration with God: "Such was the appearance of the likeness of the glory of the Lord. And when I saw it, I fell upon my face, and I heard the voice of one speaking. And he said to me, 'Son of man, stand upon your feet, and I will speak with you.' And when he spoke to me, the Spirit entered into me and set me upon my feet; and I heard him speaking to me" (Ezekiel 1:28–2:2).

Chart the responses of persons to God's Presence or absence in their lives in their conversations with you. See where they are on a gradient from one to ten from an "over-against" relationship to an "alongside" relationship. Some will shift gradually, and others will shift slowly. Then chart the process of your counseling from interview to interview to see what changes occur in the person's reports of his or her relationship to God. Not surprisingly, you will find that their "alongsideness" with you increases accordingly. Or, their "over-againstness" to the counseling relationship increases as they more and more lapse into even psychotic fear of God and neighbor. I have recorded the instance of the "contemporary Moses" in which he shifted from "over-againstness" to "alongsideness," both in relation to God and to me.

My hope for the full maturity of pastoral counseling is that we will both be called upon by others and feel called ourselves to focus intently with persons on their consciousness of the Presence of God and God's action in their lives. Spiritual direction of the ongoing stressful pilgrimages of individuals, families, and small groups is, for me, the wave of the future for pastoral counselors.

The crux of the "over-againstness" toward God is rage—what can be done with it? Underneath this is the subtle but unconfessed need to *be* God ourselves. As Nietzsche said: "There is no God. How could there be if I were not He?" This is both the theological issue in the shift or transformation of our relationship to God and the therapeutic issue in the parallel process between pastoral counselor and counselee. This shift of relationship has been called a "turning," a "conversion," a "snapping," a "peak experience," and other names over the years. I use the term "shift" because it is a relatively "connotation"-free name.

The dramatic transformation is not only a shift of human experience, but a shift in the revelation of God's Presence to us— from epiphany and theophany to incarnation. The Book of Hebrews opens with a historical summary of this shift: "In many and various ways God spoke of old to our fathers by the prophets; but in these last days he has spoken to us by a Son, whom he appointed the heir of all things, through whom also he created the world. He reflects the glory of God and bears the very stamp of his nature, upholding the universe by his word of power. When he had made purification for sins, he sat down at the right hand of the Majesty on high, having become as much superior to angels as the name he has obtained is more excellent than theirs" (Hebrews 1:1–4).

In Jesus Christ the very character of God becomes incarnate "alongside" us. He walks with us to transform us by His fellowship with us. He takes our rage, our arrogance, our self-elevation "over-against" Him into His own being. Jesus Himself never set Himself "over-against" the Father. He gave thanks that the Father always heard His prayers. He only felt grief and abandonment from God's Presence in the excruciating agony of the Cross where the wrath of the human race was unleashed against Him. In preparing His disciples for His death, He promised them the Paraclete, the Holy Spirit, as the One who would be with them always. He said He would not leave us desolate as orphans, but would come in the Holy Spirit. "If a man loves me," He said, "he will keep my word, and my Father will love him, and we will come to him and make our home with him" (John 14:23).

THE TASKS OF THE HOLY SPIRIT AND THE PASTORAL COUNSELOR

The Johannine writer and the apostle Paul report Jesus' interpretation of the tasks the Holy Spirit will perform for those whose love is centered on the Christ. The Paraclete comes "alongside" both the pastoral counselor and his or her counselee to perform these specific functions. Remarkably enough, these tasks inform what we have learned from direct experience about what effective counseling is and does. Careful attention to the biblical witness concerning the Holy Spirit in several ways *corrects* common misconceptions of pastoral counselors about our responsibilities. In other ways, it *confirms* what we have learned.

The first task of the Holy Spirit is to *teach us and call to our remembrance all that Jesus taught.* The conversations of counselees about God and the work of the Spirit of God attribute to God gruesome and hideous intentions and acts. The *memory base* of what Jesus did and taught is not there. One reason for these superstitious ideas about God is that these persons do not have in their memory what Jesus did and taught about God's love and wisdom. Yet, if he or she has "read, marked, and inwardly digested" the data of Jesus' teachings, then the *retrieval* work of the Holy Spirit works through the counselor. A pastoral counselor need not be inhibited about presenting these to the counselee. Many counselees—and pastoral counselors, also, for that matter—may say: "These I have heard from my youth up. Tell me something new." Their problems are new to them; otherwise, they would not be talking with you about them. The good pastoral counselor brings what is old, i.e., the forgotten teachings of Jesus, and sets them into the context of what is new, i.e., the hurting necessities of the counselee.

The second task of the Holy Spirit is to *bear witness to Jesus Christ.* Counselees often present reports of the work of the Holy Spirit in their lives. They ascribe much of their own magical thinking to the Holy Spirit. These thoughts are real to them, but how nearly are they in touch with reality? "Reality" is a word much used and rarely defined by psychologists, psychotherapists, marriage and family therapists, and pastoral counselors. Living in the "real" world means being able to feed, clothe, and keep one's person clean; being able to work, love, and carry out one's responsibility to family and neighbor; being relatively at peace with one's self and not a nuisance to other people. But, ethically and spiritually, the moral teachings of Jesus remembered and applied are the criteria of reality. Bearing witness to these is the work of the Holy Spirit, and apart from these people's claims about the Holy Spirit's work, they are out of touch with reality. These can be known through the Scriptures. The work of pastoral counseling is unique in that we have the hermeneutical task of relating the story of the historical Jesus to our own story and that of our counselee.[1]

The third task of the Holy Spirit is *convincing.* The Holy Spirit will "convince the world of sin and righteousness and of judgment: of sin, because they do not believe in me; of righteousness, because I go to the Father, and you will see me no more; of judgment, because the ruler of the world is judged" (John 16:8–11). The teachings of Jesus are unconvincing to large numbers of people until they become *convinced* of His crucifixion and resurrection. This is the point at which the audience at the Areopagus on Mars Hill in Athens gagged and withdrew. The sin is that "the world" rejected and crucified Christ. His righteousness *seemed* invalidated by His death, but it was vindicated in the resurrection. The rulers of the world—symbolized by Pilate—are now judged themselves.

To be convinced of this is the result of the work of the Holy Spirit now called "alongside" us. The pastoral counselor sees this in action when a counselee is convinced enough to accept the discipline of the Cross in the face of the frustration of his or her own judgment that he or she has a "right" to do as they please. As Daniel Yankelovich says: "Constant changes in commitments and outlook are not the route to real self-fulfillment. Suppression of needs is not always bad; in fact, some suppression is required if one is to avoid becoming a blob of contradictions. The Christian injunction that to find one's self one must first lose oneself contains an essential truth any seeker of self-fulfillment needs to grasp." [2]

NEW RULES

The acid question of both counselor and counselee is: Can we say "I have been crucified with Christ; it is no longer I who live, but Christ who lives in me; and the life I now live in the flesh I live by faith in the Son of God, who loved me and gave himself for me" (Galatians 2:20)? Making ethical choices upon having been convinced this way is far more than simply juggling our unconscious into consciousness. It is the conviction of having been buried with Christ in baptism and being raised to walk in the newness of life.

Intercession beyond the reach of our words is the fourth task of the Holy Spirit in which we and our counselees function "alongside" His Presence. In Romans 8:26–27 the apostle Paul says: "Likewise the Spirit helps us in our weakness; for we do not know how to pray as we ought, but the Spirit himself intercedes for us with sighs too deep for words. And he who searches the hearts of men knows what is the mind of the Spirit, because the Spirit intercedes for the saints according to the will of God." Much of pastoral counseling occurs beyond the reach of words. We intercede for our counselees as they grope to make themselves understood. The Holy Spirit intercedes for both the counselee and the counselor. One of the most repeated complaints of people in crisis is that they no longer know how to pray. This is prelude to the most profound level of communication, i.e., when language itself "plays out" and in awe-struck wordlessness both counselor and counselee rely upon the Holy Spirit to make intercession for them.

These tasks of the Paraclete are at work "alongside" the speech of the counselor and counselee. Diagnostically, we speak of "parataxic distortions," i.e., those that occur alongside the verbal output. The Presence of the Holy Spirit is the "parataxic clarifier" who enables us to begin to know as we are known by God.

The Presence of God
in the Darkness

Thou hast put me in the depths of the Pit, in the regions dark and deep. Thy wrath lies heavy upon me, and thou dost overwhelm me with all thy waves.

Psalm 88:6–7

For wicked and deceitful mouths are opened against me, speaking against me with lying tongues. They beset me with words of hate, and attack me without cause.

Psalm 109:2–3

Appoint a wicked man against him; let an accuser bring him to trial. When he is tried, let him come forth guilty; let his prayers be counted as sin!

Psalm 109:6–7

I am gone, like a shadow at evening; I am shaken off like a locust. My knees are weak through fasting; my body has become gaunt. I am an object of scorn to my accusers; when they see me, they wag their heads.

Psalm 109:23–25

Whither shall I go from thy Spirit? Or whither shall I flee from thy presence?

Psalm 139:7

If I say, "Let only darkness cover me, and the light about me be night," even the darkness is not dark to thee, the night is bright as day; for darkness is as light with thee.

Psalm 139:11–12

7
The Presence of God in the Darkness

"I do not know who God is or what God wants from me, or from anyone. I am now 28. I have struggled with despair since I was a young teenager," says a young woman. "My relationship with God is nonexistent. I have resented going to church, but have gone because of my family. I feel plagued with anger and bitterness from the past and, try as I may, it doesn't change," says a young man, age 27. Some people live their lives in quiet desperation. To them, God, if God is and is present, continually perplexes them in the dark night of their souls. St. John of the Cross speaks of this: "There is in this state (the dark night of the soul) another thing that afflicts and distresses the soul greatly, which is that, as this dark night has hindered its affections or its mind to God, neither can it pray to Him, thinking, as Jeremiah thought concerning himself, that God has set a cloud before it through which its prayer cannot pass. . . . And if it sometimes prays it does so with such lack of strength and sweetness that it thinks God neither hears it nor pays heed to it. . . ." [1]

He refers to Lamentations: "I am the man who has seen afflic-
tion under the rod of his wrath; he has driven and brought me
into darkness without any light. . . . though I call and cry for
help, he shuts out my prayer, he has blocked my ways with
hewn stones . . ." (Lamentations 3:1–2, 8–9).

The pastoral counselor, as he or she listens to people express
their real feelings about the Presence of God in their lives, hears
these kinds of expressions more often than we hear resounding
testimonies of:

> There's a glad new song ringing in my heart
> Such as angels would sing above,
> And the whole day long it doth joy impart;
> 'Tis the song of redeeming love.[2]

As we focus both our biblical and clinical learnings into one
perception of the dark night of the soul of which St. John of
the Cross speaks, three aspects appear in this struggle of the
soul in the Presence of God. First, the captivity of the person
in what John Bunyan called the "Iron Cage of Despair." Second,
the rage of the person at his or her enemies in their sphere of
personal relationships. This rage involves the bereft feeling of
abandonment and estrangement. Third, the inescapable Presence
of God in the darkness, even though God does not seem to hear
or heed their prayers, i.e., the mysterious Presence of God in
the darkness.

Martin Marty calls this bereftness from the Presence of God
the "winter of the heart" as a person cries: "O God, why dost
thou cast us off for ever?" (Psalm 74:1). In his book, *A Cry of
Absence,* he says: "The absence can . . . come . . . to the waste
space that is left when the divine is distant, the sacred is remote,
when God is silent. . . . The fury and bleakness within the soul
can remain no matter what the season or weather." [3]

It would seem that this dark night of the soul is a uniquely
Old Testament experience foreign to the Christian way of life.
This is not so. Simon Peter wept bitterly after he had denied
knowing Jesus. Prior to this, Jesus predicted Peter would be sifted
by Satan and then He prayed that he might not fail. He saw
that Peter would need a "turning again," after which He commis-
sioned him to strengthen his brethren (Luke 22:31–32). The apos-

tle Paul confessed: "We are afflicted in every way, but not crushed; perplexed, but not driven to despair. . ." (2 Corinthians 4:8). His prayer that the thorn in the flesh would be removed was not answered in the way it was asked. Before him, Jesus' Gethsemane prayer that the cup of crucifixion pass from Him was not answered. On the Cross, Jesus asked why He had been forsaken, which were the opening words of Psalm 22: "My God, my God, why hast thou forsaken me? Why art thou so far from helping me, from the words of my groaning? O my God, I cry by day, but thou dost not answer; and by night, but find no rest." (vv. 1–2).

The captivity, the rage, the bereft sense of being abandoned, and the inscrutable Presence of God in the darkness itself are inherent in both the Old and New Testament witnesses.

At least we and our counselees are not alone in the dark night of the soul. We may *think* we have been singled out by God for this agony, but this is our own need to be special, unique, and discriminated against. A whole company of other fellow strugglers surrounds us.

THE "TRAPPEDNESS"

A common theme of those who walk in darkness with the Presence of God as a "cloud of unknowing" is that they feel trapped and in need of deliverance. The Psalmist in Psalm 88 says: "Thou hast put me in the depths of the Pit, in the regions dark and deep. . . . I am shut in so I cannot escape" (Psalm 88:6, 9c).

If, as Aristotle said, life is in movement, then this person felt his or her very life was at risk because he or she had no options for living, no freedom to move this way or that, no alternatives to his or her futility. John Bunyan speaks of this trappedness in *The Pilgrim's Progress.* Mr. Interpreter took Christian by the hand again and "let him go with him into a very dark room, where there sat a Man in an Iron Cage." The man tells them: "I am now a man of Despair, and am shut up in it, as in this Iron Cage. I cannot get out. . . . I laid the reins upon the neck of my lusts . . . I have provoked God to anger, and he has left me; I have so hardened my heart that I cannot repent . . . God hath denied me repentance; his Word gives me no encouragement to believe; yea, he himself hath shut me up in this Iron Cage." [4]

The refrain of this man in the Iron Cage of Despair is repeated again and again in the stories of Protestant and Catholic counselees alike. Many believe they have committed the unpardonable sin, others will need constant reassurance that they are saved, others will make countless professions of faith, others will seek out five or six different priests a day to hear their confessions. Common to all of them is a long-standing pattern of helplessness, not only in relation to God, but also in relation to significant other persons in their lives, such as a parent, a spouse, a sibling, or a friend. In a very real way they *are* trapped in a "can't do" mode of life. They predestine themselves to "the outer darkness."

As pastoral counselors, we are often the first persons these persons seek for help. More than likely, *they* do not seek the help. Some relative or friend seeks the help *for* them. Many of these persons are people well past the age of forty. They often have had significant losses, such as the death or divorce of a spouse or the death or defection of a son or daughter who is now of age. They may be contemplating suicide, or may have already attempted suicide and did not complete the act.

A month ago, I was called to the bedside of a person who had tried desperately to kill herself. She read the Bible, but found in it only bad news. She told me almost precisely what the man in the Iron Cage of Despair told Christian. Christian asks him: "Is there no hope, but you must be kept in the Iron Cage of Despair?" The man says: "No, none at all." Christian says: "Why? The Son of the Blessed is very caring." Then the man in the Iron Cage of Despair says what my counselee said to me, almost verbatim: "I have crucified him to myself afresh, I have despised his Person, I have counted his Blood an unholy thing; I have done despite to the Spirit of Grace: Therefore I have shut myself out of all the Promises, and there now remains to me nothing but threatenings, dreadful threatenings of certain Judgment and fiery indignation, which shall devour me as an Adversary." [5]

The background Scripture for Bunyan's exceptionally accurate description is Hebrews 6:4–6. My counselee quoted this verse with great accuracy. The previous part of the paragraph in which this appears is good news, encouraging the Christian not to keep repeating over and over again the elementary phases of his or her redemption but to "go on to maturity." However, these trapped persons cannot and/or will not hear the good news. They take the words of Hebrews 6:4–6 as proof positive that they are doomed to stay trapped the rest of their lives.

Readily, one can see that the essence of Psalm 88 describes the clinical condition of a person in a profound depression. Before we had biochemical treatments for depression, these persons' despair "ran a course." They had to "sweat it out" with little or no means to expedite their recovery. The Christian community of faith has known about the care of such persons for centuries. Today, we have the advantage of skilled psychiatric care for such depressions. Patristic and medieval spiritual directors called this the "noonday sickness" after the description in Psalm 91 of "the destruction that wastes at noonday." Certain commentators assume that the author of Psalm 88 must have been suffering from some disease that drove people from him, such as leprosy. However, the modern clinical description of a unipolar depression can match the social isolation he describes without any illness.

Yet, even with antidepressant therapies of today, "sweating it out" is still very much a part of the treatment with such a person. With the best that biological psychiatric treatment and psychotherapy offers today, many such patients who are religiously concerned still live their lives in quiet desperation, feeling trapped and walled off from the grace and favor of God. Often they feel that God is "over-against" them as an enemy.

The Christian community of today and the psychiatric community, often collaboratively related to each other, can learn much from the following case record which I fortunately found in *The Records of a Church of Christ,* edited by E. B. Underhill. This record dates back to 1673, and the church was one of the Free Churches in Broadmead, Bristol, England. In 1961, I was in Bristol, England, and visited this church. A member of the church showed me the original written in beautiful longhand. I am reproducing the record here just as it was recorded by the church clerk in 1673:

Sister Mary Skinner was, after further speaking with her, and satisfaction received, added to this congregation on the sixth day of the second month, 1673.

Sister Bird, on the Key, deceased 22nd of second month, 1673, and left by will, to one of the brethren, five pounds, towards stock for the congregation.

Upon the 23rd day of this second month, 1673, a sad providence fell out to this congregation, which was this:—Our brother, John Fry, a bachelor, fell distracted. First it came upon him in a way of despairing, that he was lost and damned; then he brake out in bad language to all the brethren that came near him, calling them very bad names, and immodest expressions to some women, raving and striking them that came near to hold him, and when they were forced to bind him on the bed, he would spit at some, and use such vile and grievous words, it was consternation of spirit to all that knew him, it being so directly opposite and contrary to the whole frame of his former way and temper.

And being thus sorely assaulted and pressed by the devil, as all that beheld and heard him could not otherwise judge, he did also (and that which is worse than all) break forth into such dreadful and horrible expressions, against the whole Deity, at some times with such blasphemous words, that it made the hearts of all that heard it to ache, and the hair of their heads, as it were, to stand on end: and their spirits to be so pressed thereby hardly able to contain, or to be in the room to hear it, being so astonished at what the Lord had suffered to befall this brother; that had the testimony of all, good and bad, that he had a very lovely, humble conversation, and judged that he walked close with God, as was attested by a godly judicious doctor of physic (Dr. Ichabod Chauncey had been chaplain to Sir Edward Harley's regiment, at Dunkirk, but on the passing of the Act of Uniformity became a physician in Bristol. He was prosecuted under the 35 Eliz, and banished the realm in 1684, but returned to Bristol in 1686.—Palmer's Noncon. Mem *ii,* 352.), a member of another congregation in this city, that had lived several years tabled in the house with him, having a grave woman to his mother-in-law that kept his house, she being a sister named Fry, in fellowship with us. This doctor whilst he tabled there, observed him all along to be a very sober, practical Christian; reading and praying after the work of his outward calling (when his journeymen were departed, and his servants had left work), until the tenth and eleventh hour most nights.

His distraction broke in upon him upon the fourth day of the week (called Wednesday) and grew higher and higher, into great raging, as aforesaid. Physical means were used, but all in vain. Most persuaded he should be carried into the country for help. But some of the brethren desired the church might seek the Lord, by fasting and prayer to the Lord, to heal and deliver him.

Whereupon, the second day following, being the 28th day of the month, the congregation kept a day of prayer, in our brother Fry's house, and in the room where he was in the bed bound; but his raging was so great in the beginning of the day, that we thought we should not have been able to have continued in the room. Yet, notwithstanding, a brother began the work of the day by him, and the day was, by the Lord's assistance, carried on, and a gracious answer of prayer was given by the Lord, as we did seem to apprehend, insomuch that the spirit of rage left him in a great measure, that it ceased by the evening of that day, before we parted from him. Praise only be to the Lord!

Upon that day seven night, being the 5th day of the third month following the church came together again into the same place, and kept another day of prayer to the Lord for him. For, although the Lord did so graciously answer the church's former prayers, that in a great measure the spirit of raging left him, yet a great spirit of fear remained in him. But on this day also, the Lord did mercifully incline towards us, and gave a gracious answer to his people's seeking him in his own way; so that very observably the spirit of fear left him, that he was not so much in horror and frightful apprehensions as he had been. And means were used physically for his recovery, as blooding, purging, and leeching, to draw the distemper from his head; according to our prayers, that if the Lord pleased to have us use outward means, that he would direct to it, and bless the means; which he compassionately answered.

But when he began to come to himself, and his poor thin body, that had been plucked down, began to receive some refreshment, we had great fears his distemper would have come on again with its former violence. For though those fits ceased for above a month, yet he could not arrive to any comfort or faith, and could hardly be prevailed with to go to prayer himself; he lay under such despairing thoughts still, that it was all in vain, no promise did belong to him, etc. But he lay under reflection upon himself, what a wretch he was for what he had in or by fits uttered against, or of, the Lord. By which we perceived he remembered much, if not all; so that he was filled with such shame, that he would hide his face from every one that came to see him, or hang down his head, or not speak. He was so filled with a spirit of shame, after the spirit of rage and spirit of fear had left him, that they could not yet prevail with him to go but to a near neighbor, nor hardly to see a person that came in.

Therefore the church appointed another day of prayer for him, and so came together again, upon the ninth day of the fourth month following, anno 1673, at his house, to seek the Lord, as it were to perfect the work of his recovery, to take the spirit of shame from him, that he might go about his lawful calling forth of doors. For which the Lord gave a gracious answer of prayer also, to admiration. For the very next day after this, he was emboldened to go forth about his business in the city, as he did formerly; yea, he went from house to house, about his occasions, to his customers, for the space of four or five hours, and returned. Thus the Lord cast, as it were, three spirits, visible, to be seen, out of him: viz., a spirit of uncleanness for rage and blasphemy; secondly, a spirit of horror and fear; and thirdly, a spirit of shame, and, as it were, dumbness. Oh, the condescension, mercy, grace, favour, and faithfulness of the God and Father of our

Lord Jesus Christ, that he should answer prayer, and hear such poor, vile and unworthy ones as we were! O, nothing in us, nothing in us! Not for our sakes did he this wonderful thing in our day, but for his own name's sake; having engaged himself to do for us whatsoever we ask in the name of our Lord Jesus Christ. Laus Deo. Sola Deo gloria. Whom, to this day, near three years since he recovered, the Lord hath kept in his former glorious frame of spirit; and he usually exercises in prayer, in the congregation, on fast days, as formerly, and hath been very well ever since in his body. Magnified be the Lord!

At the very outset of this case, we are impressed with the fact that this is a *church* record and not just the record of an individual pastor. When I visited this church in England, I asked who was the pastor in 1673. I learned that the Rev. Thomas Hardcastle had come to the church in 1671, having been ejected from Bramham in Yorkshire. An engraved plaque in the vestibule of the church states that "he was imprisoned seven times for religion, and died suddenly, August 29th, 1678." It is likely, then, that at the time of the illness of Brother Fry the pastor was in prison and the church members themselves were doing the pastoral work under his supervision from the prison!

It appears that the whole church was involved in the care of Brother Fry. Members participated to the limit of their vision in an intelligent concern for him. The gathered community accepted responsibility in the total task of pastoral care. Decisions were corporate ones and not the isolated acts of a professional pastor. This points to the conclusion that pastoral care today, if theologically sound, should involve the active witness, instruction, and concern of the whole church. Short of this, pastoral care becomes just another "specialty" one more step removed from the central meaning of the witness of the church to "the whole counsel of God" in the redeeming grace of Jesus Christ. The processes of pastoral care are little more than the sewing of a new patch on an old garment unless the purpose of the church as a whole is both enlightened and implemented toward the healing witness of the ministry of love to the disturbed, spirit-possessed, and internally shattered folk such as Brother John Fry.

In the second place, we notice that the Broadmead Church was not totally agreed as to how to care for Brother Fry. "Most persuaded he should be carried into the country for help. But some of the brethren desired the church might seek the Lord, by fasting and prayer to the Lord, to heal and deliver him." The remainder of the church at least gave assent by silence. The smaller group knew the Lord had said that some healings come only by prayer and fasting. They chose to submit themselves to these disciplines. The disciplines of pastoral care today are listening, prayer, and fearless relationship. As fat and bloated as some of us are from overeating, fasting could well be added with something better than "waistline vanity" as a motive. Great numbers of people are not going to give themselves over to such disciplines for the sake of distressed people within or without the church. But the intensive disciplines of committed prayer, study, attention, and suffering are met by commensurate response from the Lord of Life who has deigned to express His healing grace through those who bring themselves into submission to His purposes.

In the third place, we observe this group of Christians turning trustingly to the medical resources they had at hand. They consulted Dr. Ichabod Chauncey, and "means were used physically for his (Brother Fry's) recovery." They prayed "that if the Lord pleased to have us use outward means, that he would direct to it, and bless the means; which he compassionately answered." Here we find the antithesis of modern "faith healers," who look upon any use of medical means of healing as something different from, other than, and even opposed to the healing work of God. God is neither restricted *to* nor *away from* the knowledge of one of His creatures in His healing of another of His creatures. For both the doctor and the patient, the disease and the medical knowledge of the disease and its cure are a part of the creation of which God is sovereign. In neither instance has God made anything common or unclean. Such attitudes are the groundwork of our intensive cooperation with medical experts in modern pastoral care. Such cooperation is not substitution for the power of God but an evangelical outreach of the church to encompass that which the Creator—God—has made available. It is an outreach that seeks to bring that cooperation into the orbit of His sovereign grace, doctor and all, just as did the Broadmead Church.

In the fourth place, the Broadmead record shows that the people of the church carefully observed the behavior of Brother John Fry. They were almost uncanny in the detail with which

they noted his "way of despairing," his muteness, his unprece-
dented change of personality from his usual pattern of life, and
the progressive phases of his illness. They discerned the spirits
qualitatively, using the primitive psychological concepts at hand,
namely, spirit-possession, with a generous mixture of down-to-
earth common sense. They traced the process of his illness in
terms of the three spirits which had possessed him: "the spirit
of uncleanness," "the spirit of horror and fear," and "the spirit
of shame."

In the fifth place, we sense the deep self-searching going on
in the lives of those who did the ministering. Without self-examination and frank admission of our own sinfulness, weakness, and
fears, no real helpfulness comes to others. This *is* prayer! And
this group of Christians admitted that they could hardly stand
it; they wanted to run! They had trouble staying in the same
room with Brother Fry. They were tempted to rebuke, to extort,
to condemn, but they did none of these! What did they do? First,
they admitted their own anxieties, fears, and self-righteousness.
Second, they listened and observed Brother Fry with prayerful,
sustained, and fearless attention. They stayed by him. Third,
they accepted him with an unconditional love. Fourth, they took
his bad behavior as a part of his total disturbance, overlooked
it, and did not judge him harshly. Finally, they believed in his
fundamental integrity and entrusted both his and their lives into
the hands of God. These four expressions of faith, hope, and
love were, in my opinion, the secret of their healing power.

Again, the Broadmead group did not feel that *they* had healed
Brother Fry when he finally came back to himself. They attributed
the act to God and to His faithfulness to keep His promises.
This is the hallmark of all pastoral care—Jewish, Catholic, or
Protestant. We are—or should be—averse to attributing any results to our own efforts. In fact, this is the fundamental distinction
between the religious and secular approaches to counseling, i.e.,
the essential humility of the counselor who attributes results,
not to our own efforts, but to the cooperative response of God
to our discipline and prayer. This puts many faith healers, however pious, into the secular camp. It puts many faithful doctors
into the religious camp. It puts many pastoral counselors—preen-
ing our feathers with a sense of personal accomplishment—to

shame! For as the Broadmead record says: "O, nothing in us, nothing in us!"

Finally, the Broadmead record does what many pastoral and medical records today fail to do; it gives us a three-year follow-up. It says that Brother Fry through "the Lord hath kept in his former glorious frame of spirit." Whether only symptoms or the real causes were dealt with, the three-year follow-up is reassuring as to results.

The "walled in" spirit was set free; the lock to the Iron Cage of Despair was broken.

THE RAGE

Lover and friend shunned the author of Psalm 88. Rage at his enemies (whom he considered to be the enemies of God, as well) filled the author of Psalm 109 in the "shadow of the evening" he felt himself to be. As Dylan Thomas said, he "raged, raged, against the dying of the light." He did not go anywhere gently. The invective he hurls against his enemies does not stop at them but extends to their families as well!

> May his children be fatherless,
> and his wife a widow!
> May his children wander about
> and beg;
> May they be driven out of the
> ruins they inhabit!

The trappedness of the person who walks in darkness from God is often pent-up rage. They suffer an "inwardness with a jammed lock" with their anger, to use Sorén Kierkegaard's metaphor. The redeeming feature of the author of Psalm 109 is that he poured out his rage to God in his prayers. Sentimental pietism in the Presence of God leaves no room for this kind of candor in prayer. Yet, the Psalmist could break out of the trappedness of his rage by pouring out his or her complaint to God directly. Yet, his prayer is an invective, also, against his enemies. Nevertheless, he could identify and describe precisely his enemies. The patient to whom I just referred could perceive doctors as her enemy, but she could not put into words or even perceive her great rage against her husband. She projected this onto God.

A more generative example of rage, however, is Hannah, described in careful detail in 1 Samuel 1:12–22. Hannah, "because the Lord had closed her womb . . . was distressed and prayed to the Lord, and wept bitterly." Eli the priest observed her mouth as she prayed. She "was speaking in her heart; only her lips moved, and her voice was not heard; therefore Eli took her to be a drunken woman. . . . But Hannah answered, 'No, my lord, I am a woman sorely troubled. . . . I have been pouring out my soul before the Lord. Do not regard your maidservant as a base woman, for all along I have been speaking out of my great anxiety and vexation.' " She let her complaints be known to God. She was rewarded for it, not rebuked. This is the first step out of the Iron Cage of Despair.

The art of pastoral counseling at this stage is to enable persons to locate and put into words before God the precise target of their rage. We can sympathize with Eli in that we, also, make some wild estimates as to what prompts such rage! At the heart of such rage is a person's wild effort to control not only his own destiny, but to be in control of all the events that happen to him. This includes resisting the authority of those to whom or for whom he or she feels responsible, such as parents, a spouse, or an employer. For example, in cases of complicated grief in which a person is enraged at God for causing the death of a loved one, I have found it helpful to suggest that this is one situation they have "come up against" over which they had no control. Are they really saying that they are enraged at being so helpless themselves?

THE PRESENCE OF GOD IN THE DARKNESS

Psalm 88 speaks of the trappedness of the human spirit in despair. It concludes by saying, as Leslie Brandt translates it: "Good Lord, where are you? Is there nothing within me worth saving?" Psalm 109 records the thunderous rage of the Psalmist at the injustices being heaped upon him or her by those around him or her. He concludes his invective with thanksgiving: "With my mouth I will give great thanks to the Lord; I will praise him in the midst of the throng. For he stands at the right hand

of the needy, to save him from those who condemn him to death"
(Psalm 109:30–31).

Psalm 139 captures the darkness itself and affirms it as a part
of the awesome mystery of the Presence of God. The knowledge
of God is totally discerning and "too wonderful for me; it is
high, I cannot attain it," this Psalmist says. The darkness is
only prelude to the deeper assurance of God's pervasive Presence:
"If I say 'Let only darkness cover me, and the light about me
be night,' even the darkness is not dark to thee, the night is
bright as the day; for darkness is as light with thee" (Psalm
139:6, 11–12).

This is very congruent with St. John of the Cross's three metaphors. His first metaphor is "the dark night." The human soul
is not able to look at the whole light of God any more than
the naked eye can safely stare into the bright sun. It was Nietzsche
who said that we would die if we were to see the whole truth
at once. In this sense, darkness is a *protective* adaptation of our
finiteness to God's infinite glory. This allows and permits "the
inflowing of God into the soul." St. John's second metaphor is
"the betrothal" in which the purified intentions of the soul can
respond safely to the impact of God's Presence. The third metaphor is the "spiritual marriage" in which God dwells in us and
we in God. Thus, the darkness is no longer an enemy, but an
intimate companion.

The whole thrust of Psalm 139 is to set aside the uncanny
fear of the darkness of mystery and of the unknown that pervades
our thinking and that of our counselees. This Psalmist insists
with Wordsworth that in mystery it is a "dark inscrutable work-
manship that reconciles discordant elements."

Our counselees, however, do not often come to us at a level
of maturity that can live at peace with mystery. They often, at
best, function at a "grammar school" level of concrete operations
in their ability to think. Everything has to be neatly classified
and ordered. Yet, they lack one of the childlike characteristics
of a "grammar school" thought life: curiosity. The sense of awe,
wonder, and mystery are the stuff of which a growing faith is
made. Rudolph Otto's perception of the Holy as the provocateur
of the feelings of *mysterium tremendum* and *mysterium fascinans*
has outlived many other attempts to put the sense of the Presence
of God into words. I think it will continue to do so.

On balance, pastoral counseling in the Presence of God is at its best in cultivating and enhancing the sense of wonder and expectancy of light as people sit in darkness. The process of pastoral counseling is much like Plato's allegory of the den in which people are trapped and bound in a cave of darkness. They can hear only echoes of persons from outside the cave behind them, and they can see only shadows of light in the darkness. Then someone comes into the darkness, loosens their bonds, and gradually leads them a little at a time as their eyes get accustomed to the light. As Plato says: "At first he will see the shadows best, next the reflections of men and other objects in the water, and then the objects themselves; then he will gaze upon the light of the moon and the stars and the spangled heaven; and he will see the sky and the stars by night better than the sun or the light by day. . . ." *The Republic,* Book VII.

The darkness, then, is not an enemy but a protection of our vision of God. God is the God of the darkness as well as the light. We are encouraged to be astronomers of the Spirit and to survey God's Presence *best* in the protection of His "dark side." Joseph knew what the Pit was. He had been thrown into it. Later, when interpreting the Pit and being sold into slavery to his brothers, he could say: "God sent me before you to preserve for you a remnant on earth, and to keep alive for you many survivors. So it was not you who sent me here, but God . . ." (Genesis 45:7–8). God was at work *for* him in his "dark night of the soul."

Minnie Louise Haskins puts into words a difficult wisdom:

> I said to the person at the gate of the year:
> "Give me a light that I may tread safely
> into the unknown."
> That person said unto me:
> "Go out into the darkness and
> Place your hand in the Hand of God.
> That will be to you better than a light
> And safer than a known way."

The Presence of God, the Presence of the Counselor, and the Face of a Parish

When Moses came down from Mount Sinai, with the two tables of the testimony in his hand as he came down from the mountain, Moses did not know that the skin of his face shone because he had been talking with God. And when Aaron and all the people of Israel saw Moses, behold, the skin of his face shone, and they were afraid to come near him.

Exodus 34:29–30

For they say, "His letters are weighty and strong, but his bodily presence is weak, and his speech of no account." Let such people understand that what we say by letter when absent, we do when present. Not that we venture to class or compare ourselves with some of those who commend themselves. But when they measure themselves by one another, and compare themselves with one another, they are without understanding.

2 Corinthians 10:10–12

Now at Lystra there was a man sitting, who could not use his feet; he was a cripple from birth, who had never walked. He listened to Paul speaking; and Paul, looking intently at him and seeing that he had faith to be made well, said in a loud voice, "Stand upright on your feet." And he sprang up and walked. And when the crowds saw what Paul had done, they lifted up their voices, saying in Lycaonian, "The gods have come down to us in the likeness of men!" Barnabas they called Zeus, and Paul, because he was the chief speaker, they called Hermes. And the priest of Zeus, whose temple was in front of the city, brought oxen and garlands to the gates and wanted to offer sacrifice with the people. But when the apostles Barnabas and Paul heard of it, they tore their garments and rushed out among the multitude, crying, "Men, why are you doing this? We also are men, of like nature with you, and bring you good news, that you should turn from these vain things to a living God who made the heaven and the earth and the sea and all that is in them. . . ."

Acts 14:8–15

8

The Presence of God, the Presence of the Counselor, and the Face of a Parish

Moses' face reflected the radiance of Yahweh in whose Presence he was and had been. "Face" is a metaphor for the Presence of God, and is also a metaphor for the whole personality of Moses. He was not aware "that the skin of his face did shine."

In the New Testament, Paul and Barnabas healed a man who was a cripple from his birth and had never walked. The people spoke in their own tongue and said: "The gods have come down to us in the likeness of men!" The two apostles were shocked to learn that Barnabas was perceived to be Zeus, the Greek deification of the shining sky, the elements of rain, thunder, and lightning. Paul was considered by them as being Hermes, the messenger of Zeus, his spokesperson.

Paul and Barnabas obviously had an overpowering presence of their own derived from their relationship to God. They were not aware of it until the people sought to deify them in the form of the gods of the Greeks. Then Paul said: ". . . why are you doing this? We also are men, of like nature with you, and bring you good news, that you should turn from these vain things to a living God who made the heaven and the earth and the sea and all that is in them." Yet, "with these words they scarcely constrained the people from offering sacrifice to them" (Acts 14:15, 18). Not only does the Presence of God pervade all our relationships. Being in that Presence generates changes in us that make our beings a "presence" in our own right, as well.

Paul's presence did not always evoke such adulation and deification. The Corinthians to whom he wrote apparently were overwhelmed by his letters. He said to them that he did not want to frighten them with his letters. Nevertheless, they disparaged his personal "presence." They said: "His letters are weighty and strong, but his bodily presence is weak, and his speech is of no account." To say the least, in well-worn pastoral counseling jargon, they expressed both positive and negative transference feelings toward him. They were ambivalent! He was coming to terms with them as to what his presence meant *to them*.

In fact, this is the whole *raison d'etre* of the Second Letter to the Corinthians. He writes his *apologia pro vita sua,* that is, his defense of his life as an apology, not in the sense of confessing some wrong, but an apology as a *defense* of his ministry. Earlier in the Epistle, he had said that the light of the knowledge of God had been made known to people in the face of Jesus Christ. In this passage, he is "facing" them with the meaning of his own "presence" among them. They are "facing up" to his presence and the power of the gospel about which he wrote.

REAPPRAISING THE "TRANSFERENCE"

We contemporary pastoral counselors can break through to the transcendent and transpersonal dimensions of our relationship to our counselees by becoming less pedestrian and trivial in our awareness of *who* it is of whom we remind our counselees. Thus, we as pastoral counselors remind them of their father, mother, brother, sister, and so on. This is usually described as "the transference." The unconscious process of *transference* is operative in every human relationship. Beginning with Freud, this phenomenon has meant that ideas or impressions in the conscious and preconscious mind, left to themselves, "establish a connection between it and (an) unconscious wish, and transfer to it the energy of the unconscious wish." [1] Thus, fantasies and wishes from the distant past, such as the wish to kill one's father, to possess him completely in sexual union, breaks into consciousness to distort and confuse the relationship to an employer, or the therapist, or someone else.

Far more than this, we remind them of whatever they perceive God to be. Their perceptions of God are confirmed, corrected, denied, or reassessed in the process of being in our presence. We need to keep clearly in mind Anton Boisen's critique of Freud's dogma that God is a projection of the infantile responses of a person to his or her parents. Boisen said that, to the contrary, the parents drew their "godlike" presence from the Eternal God. The child will be restless until he or she has come to know the Eternal and not just the shadows and echoes of the Eternal he or she experiences in parents, teachers, counselors, and therapists.

Separating the reality of God from these distortions is the work of pastoral counseling. Correspondingly, the pastoral counselor is presumptuous to assume that he or she can or should try to be *the sole* arbiter of confused transferences. When he or she is expected to be the *sole* arbiter, both the counselor and the counselee are ambushed by their feelings of the *absence* of God. The parental and sibling images become idols. But, as Ralph Underwood aptly says: "The presence of God creates prayer; the absence of God necessitates prayer." [2] He encourages us to perceive the absence of God as a clue to the presence: ". . . today religion is becoming so privatized that people often lack courage to speak to others candidly about either God's presence or absence in their lives." [3] It is just easier, I would say, to speak of father, mother, brother, or sister.

One of the least defined and most used terms in psychological, psychiatric, and psychoanalytic conversations about transference is the word "reality." The function of the ego in psychoanalytic terms is "reality-testing," but what *is* the reality being tested? Ordinarily, reality means the correspondence of a person's conception or perception of what they see or hear with what is actually "out there." Their perception is not "distorted" but accurate. In this sense, the "transference" is better described by Harry Stack Sullivan's term, "parataxic distortion." He defines this as "the interviewee's substituting for the psychiatrist a person or persons strikingly different in most respects from the psychiatrist.

The interviewee addresses his behavior toward the reality of the psychiatrist, and he interprets the psychiatrist's remarks and behavior on the basis of this same fictitious person." [4]

I note the phrase, "the reality of the psychiatrist." It seems that the psychiatrist here *is* reality. In humanism, man is the measure of all things. In this setting, the psychiatrist himself or herself is the measure of all things—reality. He or she is being distorted in the perception of the interviewee. The person or persons being substituted for by the psychiatrist seem to have an omnipresence and omnipotence that overflows the person's *mitwelt,* or world of other persons. In turn, the objective of the therapy is that the therapist serves as a "new model of reality." This enables the patient to compare his or her feelings and attitudes with those of the therapist, note the differences, and respond differently. He or she is encouraged to "lower the importance" of the fictitious person for whom they have mistaken the physician and to see them as they are, ordinary mortals and not gods in the form of men or women.

This focuses our discussion more pointedly on the distinctive definition of "reality" inherent in *pastoral* interventions in people's lives. Much pastoral counseling theory simply accepts the psychoanalytic truism about the therapist *as* reality. Clear expositions of what or who reality is are as scarce and poorly defined in pastoral counseling literature as in psychiatric literature. The same fictitious responses or distortions of which Sullivan speaks occur in the pastoral relationship. However, reality in a pastoral sense is the Eternal Presence, not the pastor himself or herself. Yet, this does not mean that the pastor is not a presence in his or her own right. He or she is. The counselee also has a presence, a bearing, and identity of his or her own, as well. Daniel Day Williams describes Christ as *the* reality in every human relationship. Christ is the Third Person in the pastoral relationship who discloses reality to both the counselor and the counselee about our humanity in its need and in its hope.[5] The uniqueness of pastoral counseling, it seems to me, rests in the explicit and articulate ways in which the pastoral counselor invites, includes, and interprets the Third Presence of Christ in what otherwise would be a purely humanistic interpretation of the transference situation.

Pastoral counseling, when the person doing it explicitly perceives reality to be the Christ, does not move on the assumption that the pastoral counselor *is* reality. To the contrary, he or she is a person of like nature with the counselee, a fellow struggler. We have this ministry in "earthen vessels, to show that the transcendent power belongs to God and not to us" (2 Corinthians 4:7). Both counselor and counselee "see in a mirror dimly." We are always seeking a "face to face" meeting in which we "with unveiled face, beholding the glory of the Lord, are being changed into his likeness from one degree of glory to another" (2 Corinthians 3:18). Both pastoral counselor and counselee are at work in "seeing God as he *is.*" Both have distortions of perception.

The shift of transference and counter-transference to the transcendental power of the Presence of Christ as the Third Presence in the counseling relationship accomplishes three intensely necessary results.

First, it releases us and our counselees from the deadly trap of a dangerous kind of legalism inherent in psychologisms which James Cox accurately calls "the perfectionism of a ceaselessly touted normality." [6] In our psychological enthusiasms we as pastoral counselors tend to lose historical perspective. Yet, the history of Christian doctrine when remembered by us even subliminally gives us a feeling of *deja vu* when we see the persons we are counseling heavily laden with the hope that they will be perfectly free of any psychological "problems." They "work hard" in "working through" each immature misperception. Running through interview after interview is a schema of expectation that psychological perfection, maturity, or normality are possible for them to achieve.

The pastoral counselor's *deja vu* takes us back to Paul's admonition to the antinomians who felt that redemption in Christ gave them liberty to "sin all the more that grace might abound." Also, the Letter to the Galatians spoke to people who had difficulty accepting the grace of Christ and felt that they had to observe all the perfectionistic demands of the Jewish Law to be acceptable as Christians.

Second, shifting the focus of our counseling to the Third Presence creates a fellowship of suffering between us and our counselee. Our common humanity with them replaces both our need to "play god" and the counselee's need to place us on a pedestal at best and to deify us at worst. The "stickier" aspects of purely sexual dimensions of transference and countertransference are brought under the ethical scrutiny of the Presence of Christ, richly informed by the record of His ethical teachings. Even Freud himself, without reference to the Presence of God, points out that the physician does not accept confused sexual overtures of a female patient because she must "learn from him" how to forego the satisfaction of immediate sexual pleasure "in favour of a more distant one, which is perhaps altogether uncertain, but which is both psychologically and socially unimpeachable." [7]

Pastoral counselors have even a higher reason for doing this same thing. What we do is done in the Presence of the Third Person, the Christ, who died for this individual! Pastoral counseling done with an explicit awareness of the Third Presence of the Christ in the relationship, then, creates a down-to-earth humility in the counselor. He or she "holds fast" to his or her "good confession," as Hebrews 4:14 puts it. We and our counselee have a priest who is able to sympathize with our weaknesses and imperfection. We can both with confidence draw near to His grace to find help in time of need. We can deal gently with the ignorance and waywardness of counselees because we ourselves are beset with weakness. We, therefore, confess our own weakness as we lead the counselee in confession to God.

Third, if the pastoral counselor has sustained and developed a dynamic relationship to a church of his or her own and to other churches of the community, then he or she can "distribute" the great forces of transferred emotions of counselees to a larger family of the human community. An ordered systems approach to the family and the life of the church is a stronger representation of reality than any one therapist can be.

The end result of this down-to-earth humility in the practice of pastoral counseling is an aura, a distinctive atmosphere of trust, reverence, and contemplation surrounding our persons. We are unaware of this, even as Moses was unaware that his face did shine. The effective pastoral counselor who spends years (ordinarily in the same community) in the faithful "trialogue" of the three presences—the counselor, the counselee, and the Third Presence of Christ—develops a "weight of being," that is, he or she "carries a lot of weight" with persons in the community in which he or she works. People "turn to" him or her with an almost mystical confidence. He or she becomes a "presence" in the community. One might use another word for it—people know that this person lives out his or her life "before God." He or she carries an authentic *integrity* that is a healing grace in and of itself. The capacity he or she has to mediate peace, insight, or change in other people's lives *resides* in him or her but it *originates* from the Third Presence.

THE PRESENCE OF GOD IN THE ECCLESIA

The influence of such a presence on the part of the pastoral counselor creates a community of people. The pastoral counselor of today most often mediates such care to people on a one-to-one, family, or small group basis. Crowds rarely throng around these people. Yet, when a person has worked faithfully and consistently as a pastoral counselor in the same community over a few decades, an invisible community of those to whom he or she has been a counselor emerges. These people have a way of getting to know who each other are, quite apart from any organizational effort on the part of the pastoral counselor. They become a network of people who are concerned about other people. They have a special sensitivity for other people when they are going through deep waters of trouble. Sometimes they form themselves into spontaneous social groupings, finding their ways into the study groups, Sunday school classes, and worship services of a wide spectrum of church life in the community. In individual, family, or small group sessions, they "break the news" of these affiliations to the pastoral counselor. He or she wisely supports, sustains, and encourages "every good work" that is happening in these manifestations of a spontaneous ecclesia. He or she is awed by the growth of an ecclesia that transcends sectarian lines and disregards social class and racial lines. It is an organism, not an organization. It was not promoted. It happened.

The life of the churches cannot be left to such serendipity entirely, but in many instances the New Testament churches seemed to come into being much in this fashion. Definite planning and programming is of utmost importance in the nurturing of the church in the community. Yet, what I am saying is that the adventitious, serendipitous happening of relationships born out of shared suffering such as I have described is the beating heart of a church worthy of the name of our Lord Jesus Christ. We pastoral counselors do our work in the workweek between

Sundays. We are not nearly as visible in the churches of the community as we could be. Nevertheless, the invisible building of the ecclesia of the people of God does happen through our work. As we walk along some Emmaus road with a counselee, suddenly we are not alone. The Living Christ is with us. He opens our eyes to the meaning of the Scriptures and our hearts burn within us. The ecclesia is enlivened and the parishes are enriched.

In Georges Bernanos's *The Diary of a Country Priest,* the young priest in his first parish writes these words in his notebook: "Already three months. . . . This morning for my parish. . . . My parish! The words cannot even be spoken without a soaring kind of love. . . . I know that my parish is a reality, that we belong to each other for all eternity: it is not an administrative fiction, but a living cell in the everlasting Church. But only if God would open my eyes and unseal my ears, so that I might behold the face of my parish. The look in the eyes . . . these would be the eyes of all Christianity, of all parishes—perhaps of the poor human race itself. Our Lord saw them from the Cross . . ." [8]

The Church has been made too much an administrative or geographical fiction. Pastoral counseling itself can go in the same direction. But once we as pastoral counselors become aware of the "face" of our invisible parish, to look in its eyes would prompt us always to look at no person from a purely human point of view again. We would see each counselee as persons for whom the Third Presence in our counseling situations died, as a part of people who minister to others as we do—as wounded healers. An esteemed mentor and teacher of mine was Ray Petry, Professor of Church History at Duke Divinity School. He often said to a class as the semester ended: "Ailing physicians are we all, students. But we *will do,* for God has chosen us to do so!"

Notes

Chapter 1

1. Francis Thompson, "The Hound of Heaven." In: *A Treasury of Great Poems.* Ed. by Louis Untermeyer. New York: Simon and Schuster, 1955, 1002.
2. Howard Clinebell, *Growth Counseling.* Nashville: Abingdon Press, 1979, 126.
3. Martin Luther, *Letters of Spiritual Counsel.* Ed. by Theodore Tappert. Philadelphia: Westminster Press, 1955, 27.

Chapter 2

1. Elizabeth Nowell, Ed., *The Letters of Thomas Wolfe.* New York: Charles Scribners Sons, 1956, 83.
2. This is my one-sentence summary of Harry Stack Sullivan's point of view found in his book, *The Interpersonal Theory of Psychiatry.* New York: W. W. Norton, 1953, 308–10.
3. Alfred C. Kinsey, Wardell Pomeroy, and Clyde Martin, *Sexual Behavior in the Human Male.* Philadelphia: W. B. Saunders Co., 1948, 544. "A preliminary examination of the six thousand marital histories in this study, and of nearly three thousand divorce histories, suggest that there may be nothing more important than a determination that it shall persist. With such a determination, individuals force themselves to adjust and to accept situations which would seem sufficient grounds for a break-up if the continuation of the marriage were not the prime objective."
4. The original contribution of Sigmund Freud to the practice of any kind of religious faith is a neglected treasure for any pastoral counselor. His assessment of the obsessive compulsion in the disorders of religious scrupulosity are abundantly helpful in either the Protestant or Catholic practice of hearing people's confession of sin. See Freud's positive statement of the creative function of religion, which is worthy of using as a criterion for assessing the prophetic credibility of a given religious faith. In his paper on "From the History of an Infantile Neurosis" (1914), he wrote: ". . . it may be said that in the present case religion achieved all the aims for the sake of which it is included in the education of the individual. It put a restraint

upon his sexual tendencies by affording them a sublimation and a safe moor-
ing; it lowered the importance of his family relationships, and thus protected
him from the threat of isolation by giving him access to the great community
of mankind" (Sigmund Freud, "From the History of an Infantile Neurosis"
(1914). *The Standard Edition of the Complete Psychological Works of Sigmund Freud.* Tr. & Ed. by James Strachey. Volume XVII. (1917–1919).
London: The Hogarth Press and The Institute of Psycho-Analysis, 1955,
114–15. A remarkably clear assessment of the deleterious effects of the Ameri-
canization of Freud's thought is Bruno Bettelheim's book, *Freud and Man's
Soul.* New York: A. A. Knopf, 1982.

5. Samuel Terrien, *The Elusive Presence: The Heart of Biblical Theology.* New
York: Harper and Row, 1978, xiii. In my estimation, this book is the definitive
book on the biblical data undergirding the present concern for the "heart
of pastoral counseling." Other works I have found indispensable in my quest
have been Martin Marty, *A Cry of Absence: Reflections for the Winter of
the Heart* (New York: Harper and Row, 1983); the biography, *The Seven
Mountains of Thomas Merton* by Michael Mott (Boston: Houghton Mifflin
Co., 1984); Douglas Steere, *On Listening to Another* (New York: Harper
and Row, 1955); and Douglas Steere, *On Being Present Where You Are*
(Philadelphia: Pendle Hill Publications, 1967).
6. As quoted by Michael Mott, *The Seven Mountains of Thomas Merton.* Boston: Houghton Mifflin Co., 1984, 433.

Chapter 3

1. Emil Brunner, *Man in Revolt.* Philadelphia: Westminster Press, 1947, 96.
2. *Ibid.,* 96.
3. *Ibid.,* 345.
4. Sigmund Freud, "Observations on Transference-Love (Further Recommendations on the Technique of Psycho-Analysis III)" *The Standard Edition
of the Complete Psychological Works of Sigmund Freud.* Tr. & Ed. by James
Strachey. Volume XII. (1911–1913). London: The Hogarth Press and The
Institute of Psycho-Analysis, 1958, 169–70.
5. Henry Beveridge, Tr., *The Institutes of the Christian Religion.* Grand Rapids,
Mich.: Wm. B. Eerdmans Publishing Co., 1957. Vol. I, Ch. XI, Sec. 8, 97.

Chapter 4

1. Paul Tournier, *A Place for You.* New York: Harper & Row, 1968.
2. *Ibid.*
3. Edmund Husserl, *Ideas: General Introduction to Pure Phenomenology.* New
York: Collier Books, 1962, 427–28.
4. Andras Angyal, *Neurosis and Treatment: A Holistic Theory.* New York:
John Wiley & Sons, 1965, 93–94.

Chapter 5

1. Samuel Terrien, *The Elusive Presence: The Heart of Biblical Theology.* New
York: Harper and Row, 1978, 232.

2. *Ibid.*, 235.
3. Norman Habel, *The Book of Job.* Philadelphia: Westminster Press, 1985, 134.
4. Douglas Steere, *On Listening to Another.* New York: Harper and Brothers, 1955, 6.

Chapter 6

1. See Charles V. Gerkin, *The Living Human Document: Re-Visioning Pastoral Counseling in a Hermeneutical Mold.* Nashville: Abingdon Press, 1983.
2. Daniel Yankelovich, *New Rules: Searching for Self-Fulfillment in a World Turned Upside Down.* New York: Bantam Books, 1982, 236.

Chapter 7

1. St. John of the Cross, *The Dark Night of the Soul.* Tr. by E. Allison Peers. New York: Doubleday, 1959, 115.
2. "There's a Glad New Song." Words by Albert Fisher, © Copyright 1956. Renewal 1984 Broadman Press. All rights reserved. Used by permission.
3. Martin Marty, *A Cry of Absence: Reflections for the Winter of the Heart.* New York: Harper and Row, 1983, 2.
4. John Bunyan, *The Pilgrim's Progress.* Mount Vernon, N.Y.: The Peter Pauper Press, n.d., 34–36.
5. *Ibid.*

Chapter 8

1. Sigmund Freud, "The Interpretation of Dreams." From: *The Basic Writings of Sigmund Freud.* Tr. by A. A. Brill. New York: The Modern Library, 1938, 530.
2. Ralph L. Underwood, "The Presence of God in Pastoral Care Ministry." From: *Austin Presbyterian Theological Seminary Bulletin.* Faculty Edition. "Prayer and Pastoral Care." Vol. 101, No. 4, October, 1985, 7.
3. *Ibid.*
4. Harry Stack Sullivan, *The Psychiatric Interview.* New York: W. W. Norton, 1954, 26.
5. Daniel Day Williams, *The Minister and the Care of Souls.* New York: Harper, 1961, 67, 70.
6. James Cox, *Preaching.* New York: Harper and Row, 1985, 31.
7. Sigmund Freud, "Observations on Transference-Love (Further Recommendations on the Technique of Psycho-Analysis III)." *The Standard Edition of the Complete Psychological Works of Sigmund Freud.* Tr. & Ed. by James Strachey. Volume XII. (1911–1913). London: The Hogarth Press and The Institute of Psycho-Analysis, 1958, 169–70.
8. Georges Bernanos, *The Diary of a Country Priest.* London: Collins (Fontana Books), 1937, 28.

Index